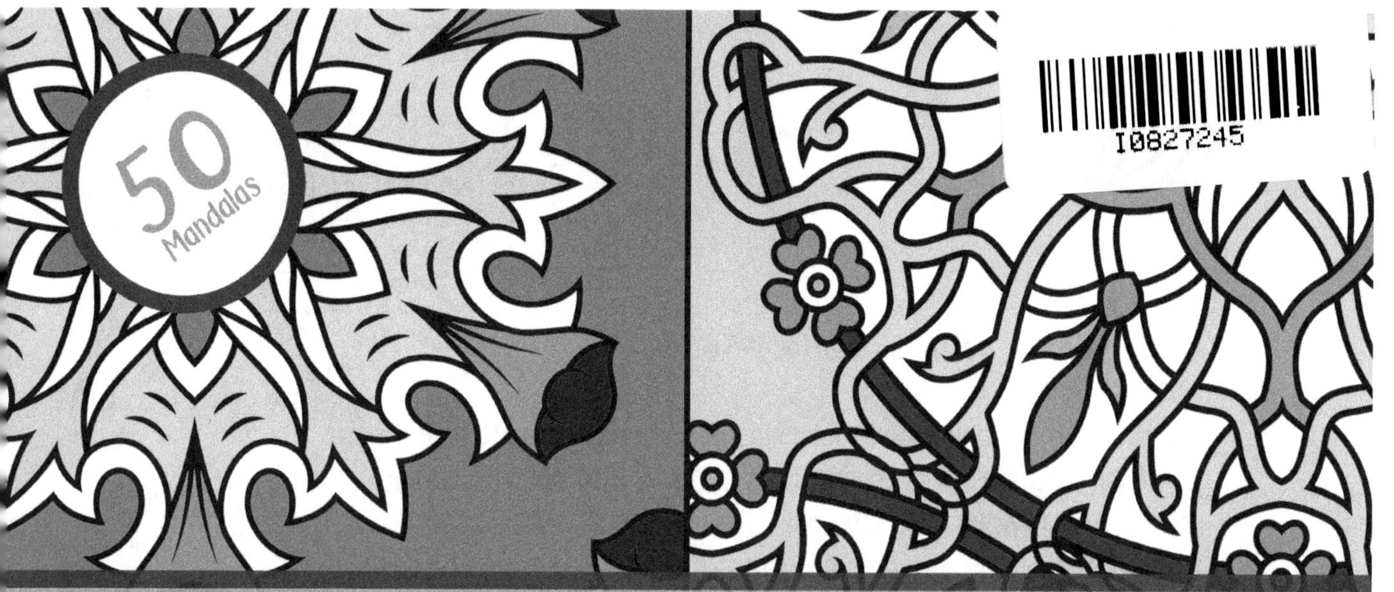

MAGNIFICENT MANDALAS ADULT COLORING BOOK 2

MANDALA MEDITATION FOR ADULTS RELAXATION & STRESS RELIEF

Kat Mariaca

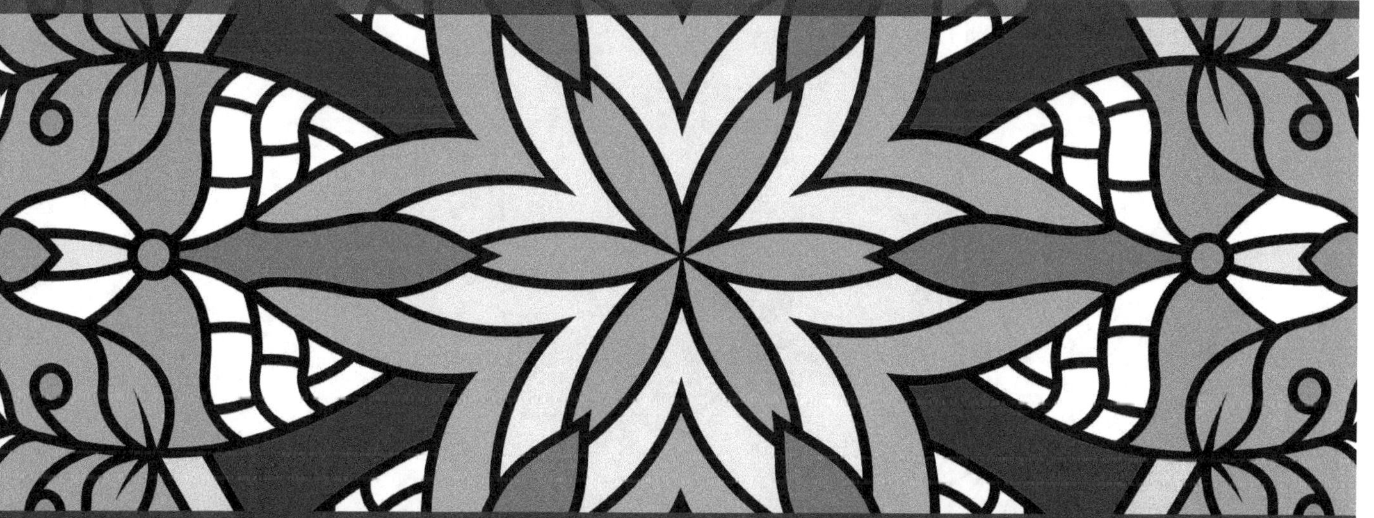

Zen & The Art of Coloring Yourself Calm Adult Coloring Books (Volume 7)

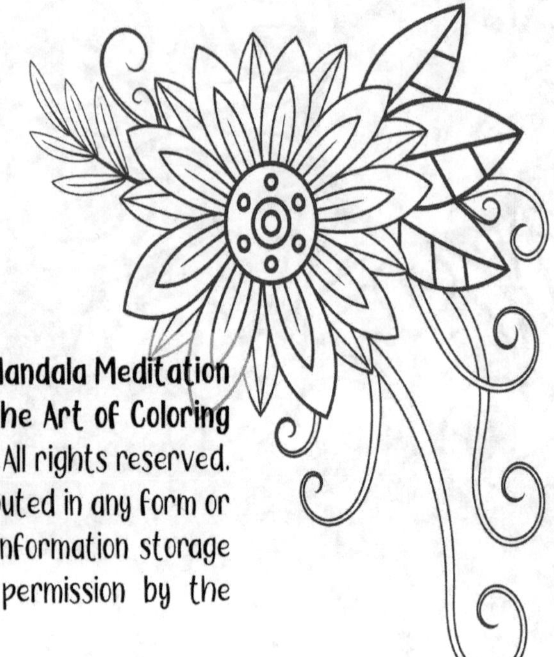

MadaketLanePublishers@comcast.net

Mariaca, Kat
Magnificent Mandalas Adult Coloring Book 2 - Mandala Meditation for Adults Relaxation & Stress Relief: Zen & The Art of Coloring Yourself Calm Adult Coloring Books (Volume 7)
1. Crafts & Hobbies 2. Nature & Plants - Flowers
3. Inspiration & Personal Growth

ISBN: 978-1-940892-25-2

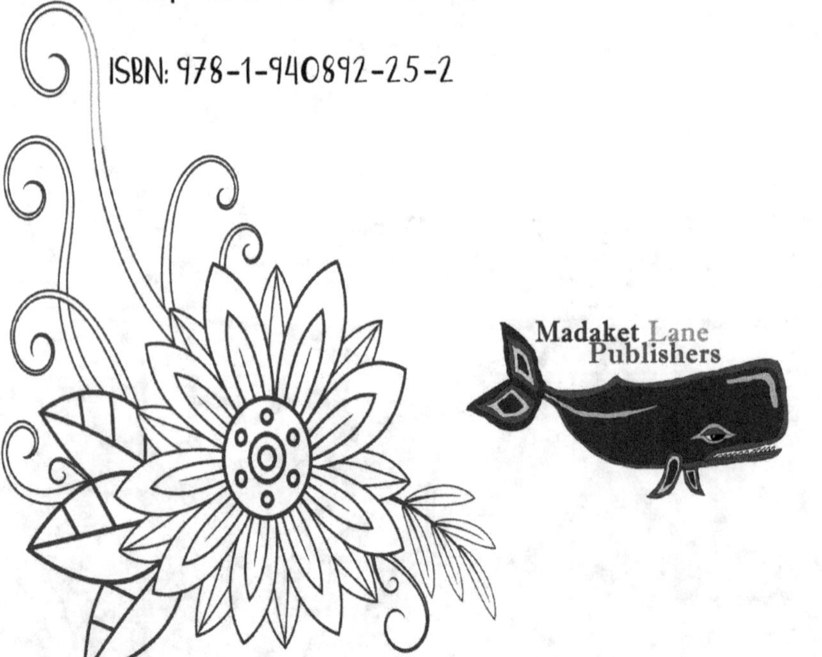

This is a Test Page

Every paper reacts differently to different mediums. Take the opportunity to test your markers, crayons, pencils, gel pens, etc. here to see how they work on this paper – test for blendability (is that a word?), bleed, and layering, as well as vibrancy and color accuracy. Note – it's always a good idea to place a sheet of paper, or even wax paper, behind the page you are currently working on so nothing will bleed through to the following pages.

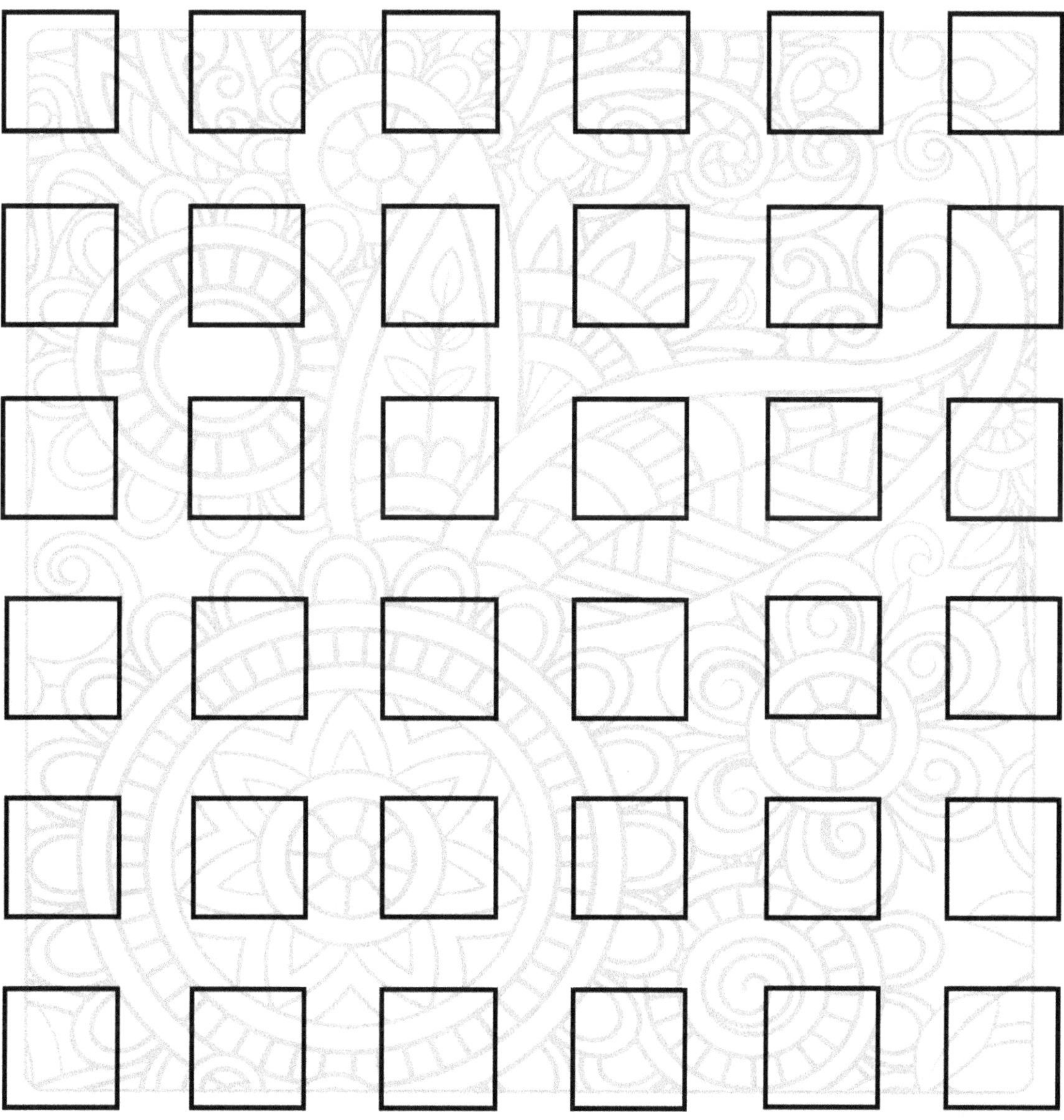

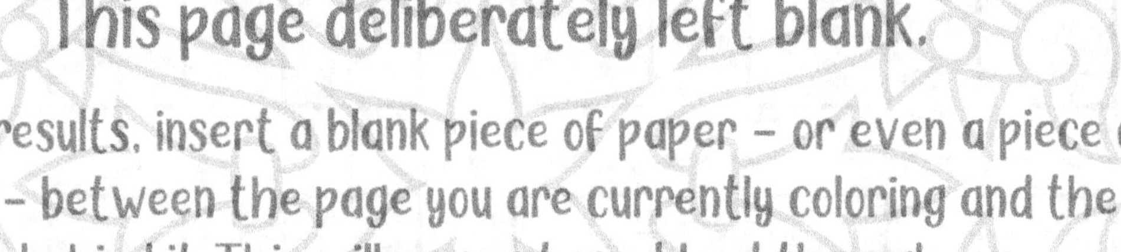

This page deliberately left blank.

For best results, insert a blank piece of paper – or even a piece of wax paper – between the page you are currently coloring and the one behind it. This will prevent any bleed through.

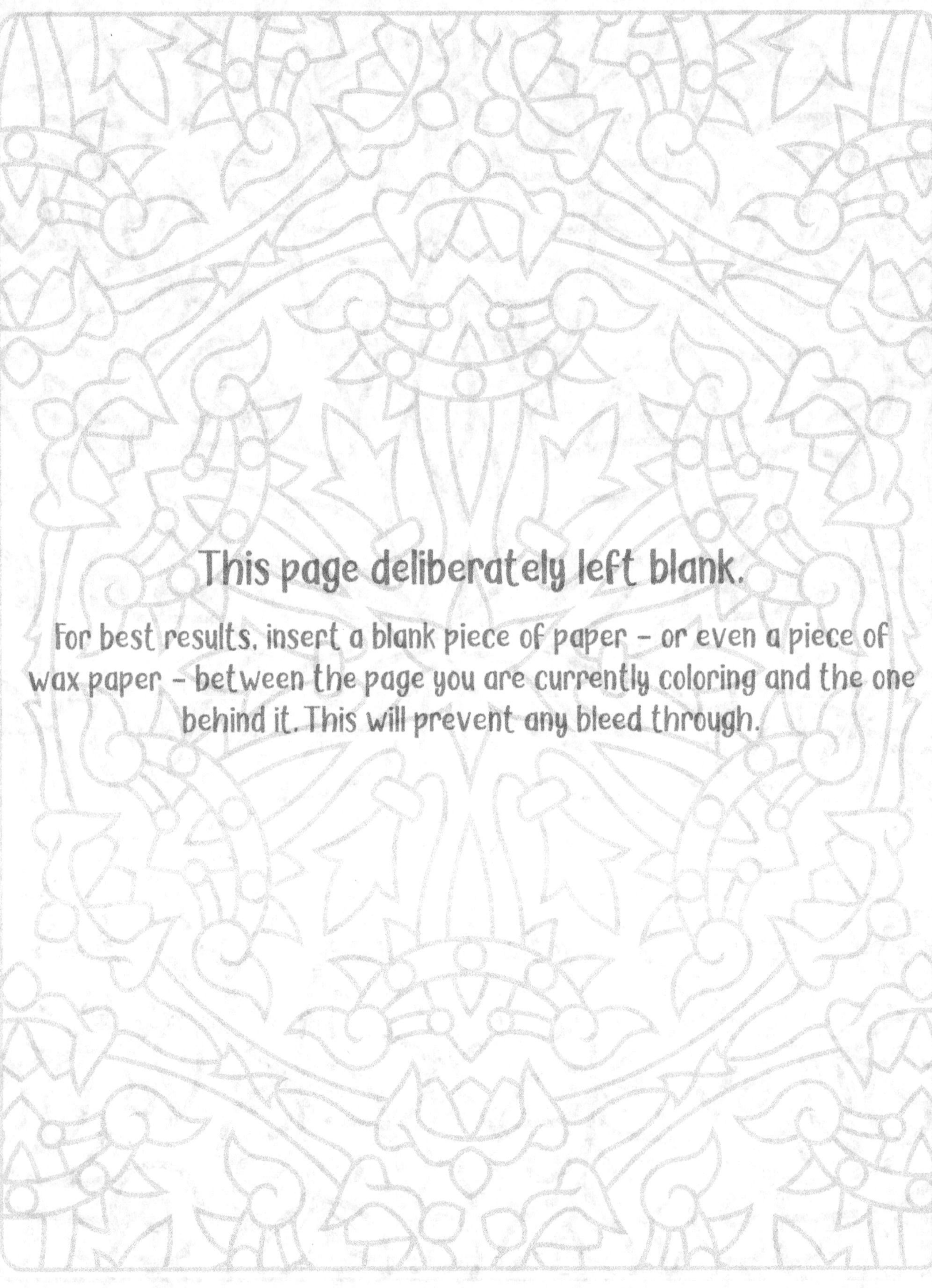
This page deliberately left blank.
For best results, insert a blank piece of paper – or even a piece of wax paper – between the page you are currently coloring and the one behind it. This will prevent any bleed through.

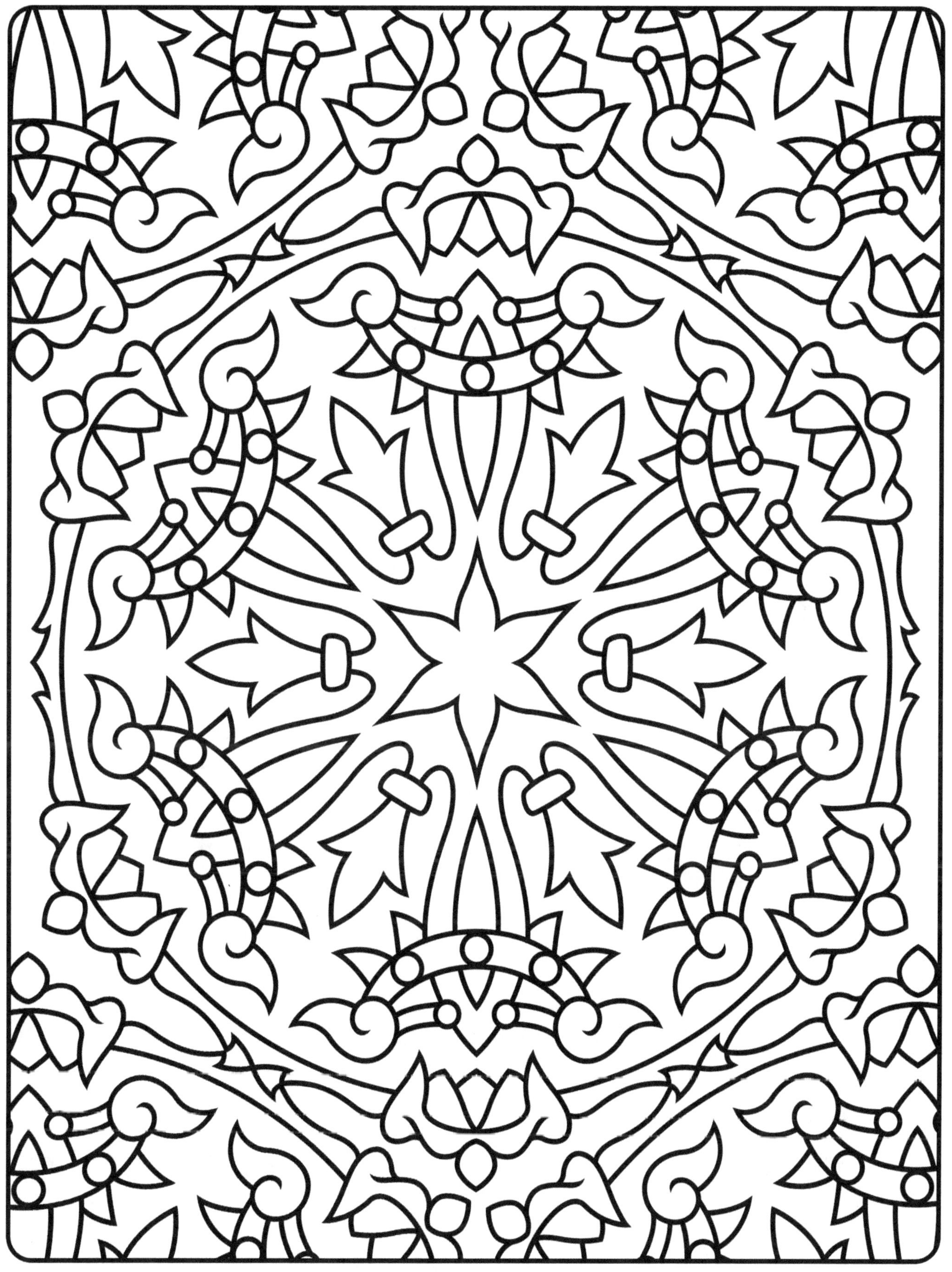

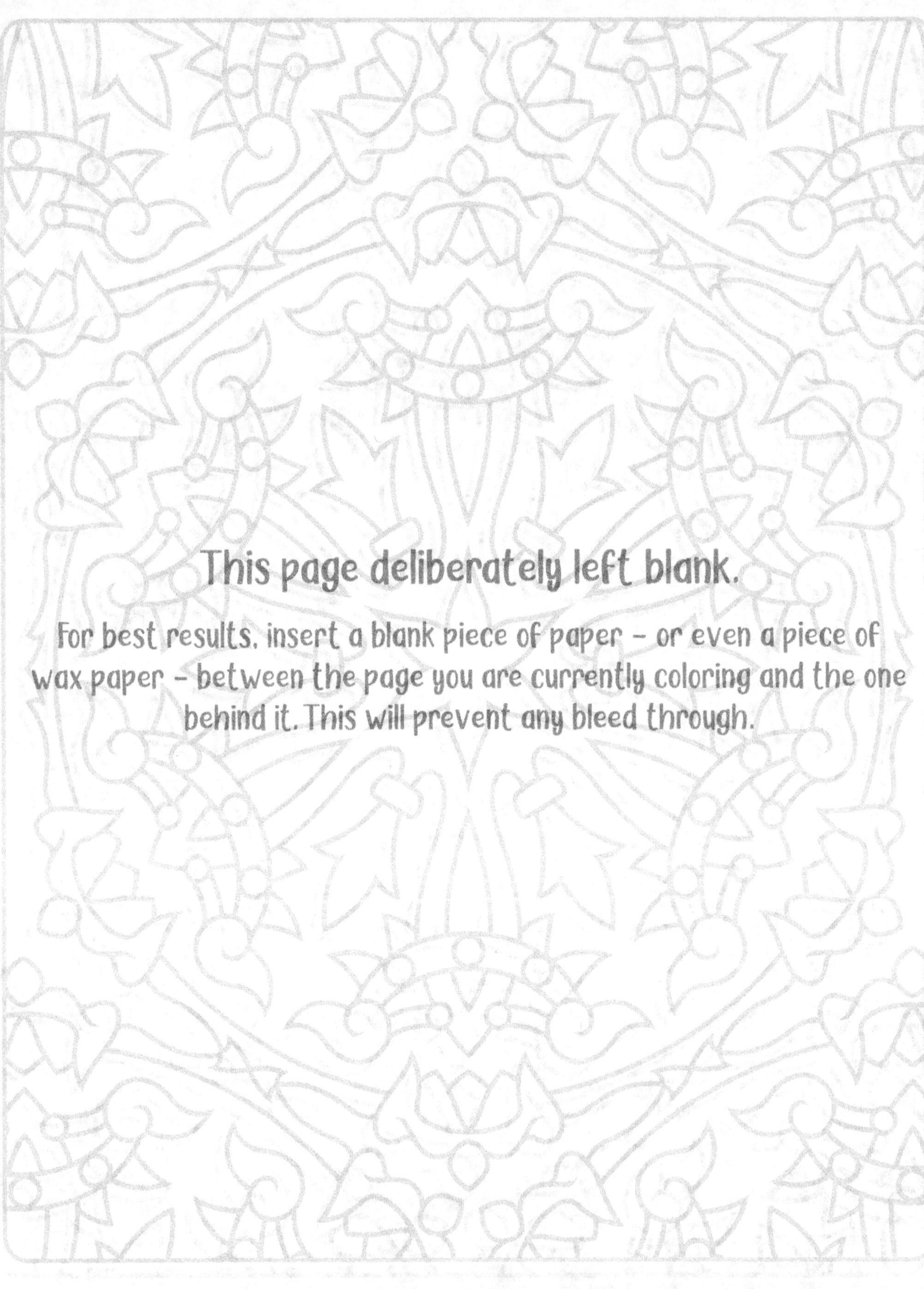

This page deliberately left blank.

For best results, insert a blank piece of paper – or even a piece of wax paper – between the page you are currently coloring and the one behind it. This will prevent any bleed through.

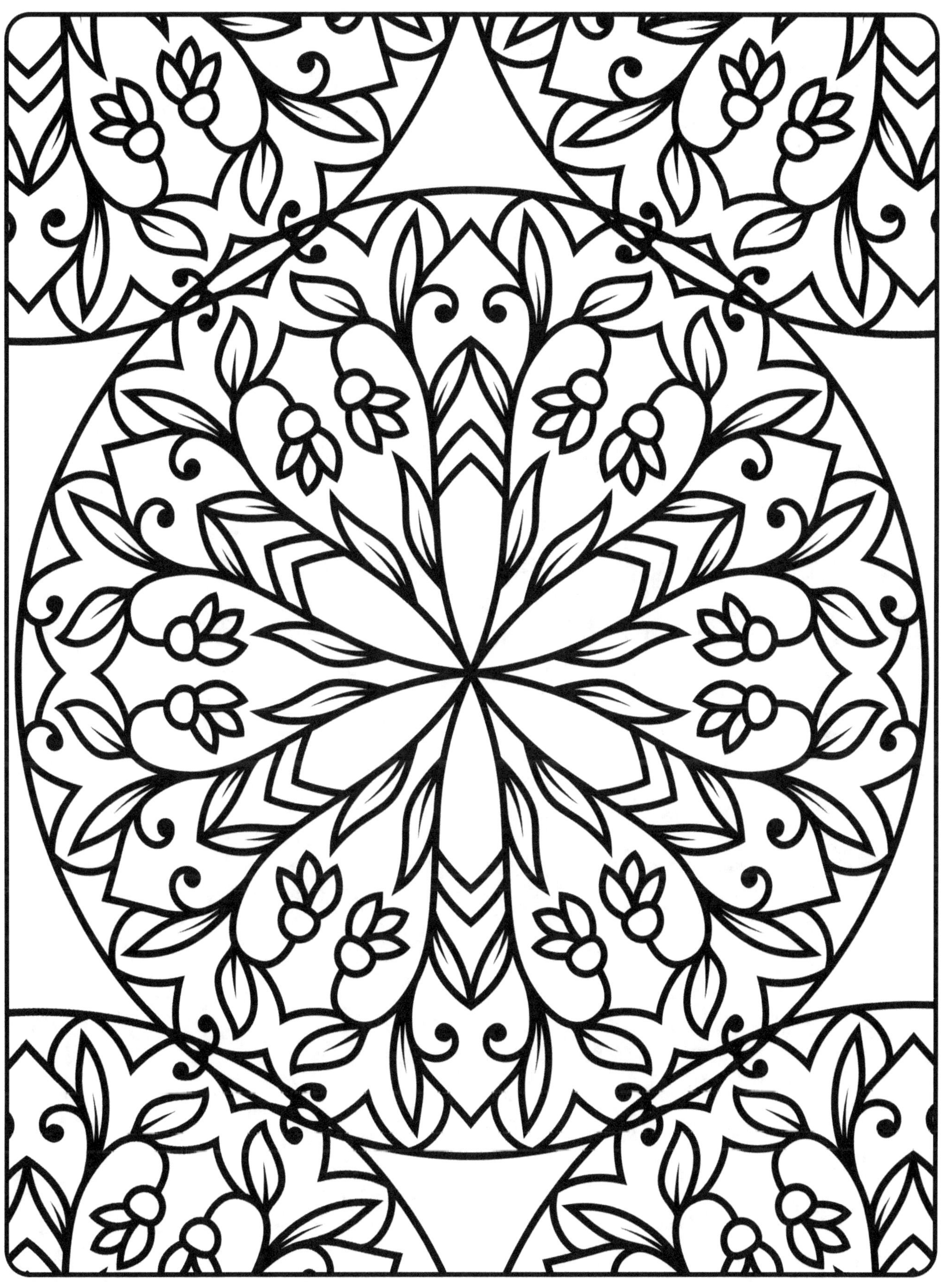

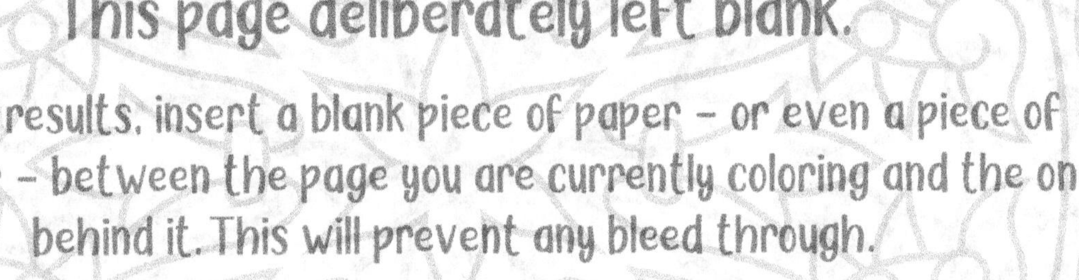

This page deliberately left blank.

For best results, insert a blank piece of paper – or even a piece of wax paper – between the page you are currently coloring and the one behind it. This will prevent any bleed through.

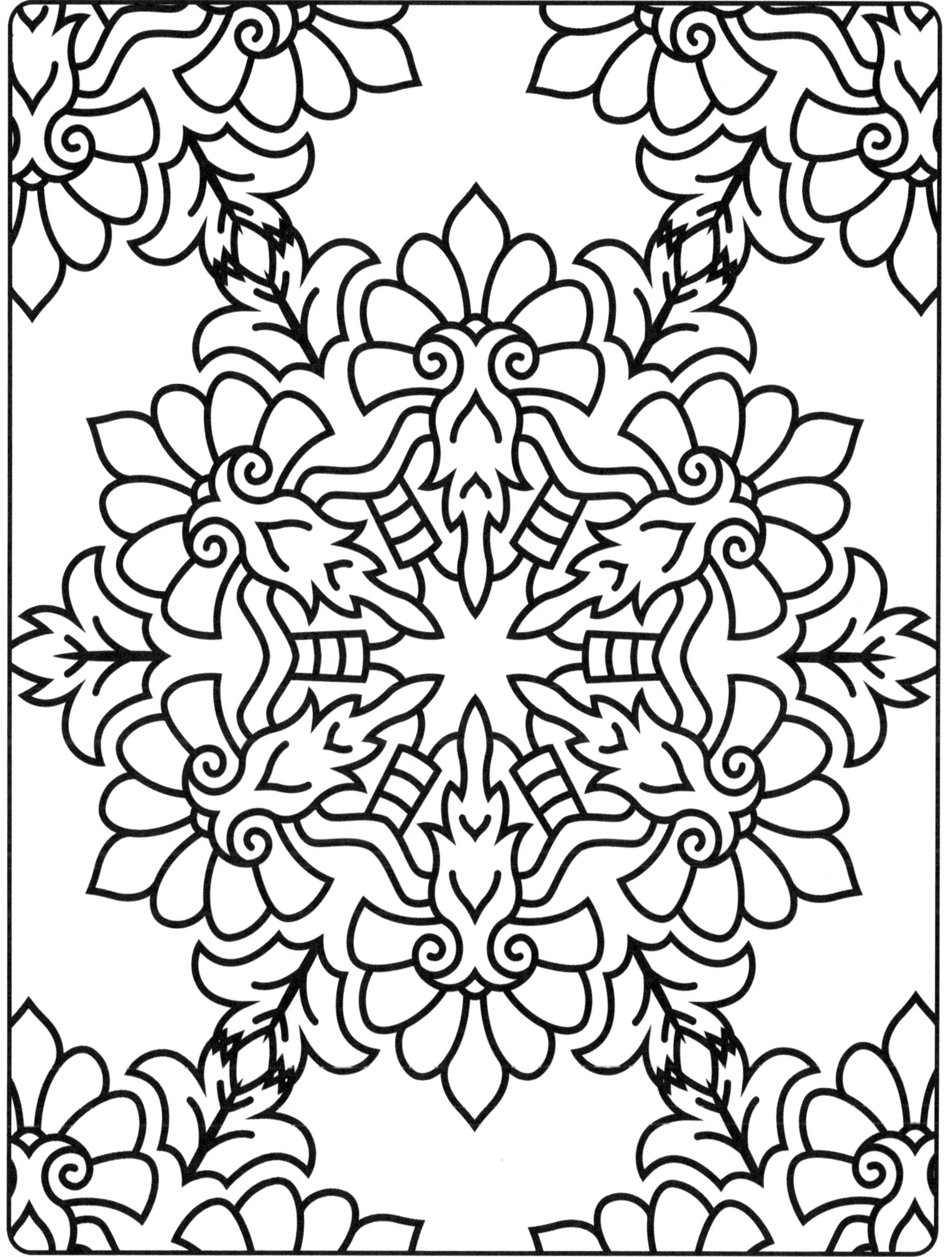

This page deliberately left blank.

For best results, insert a blank piece of paper – or even a piece of wax paper – between the page you are currently coloring and the one behind it. This will prevent any bleed through.

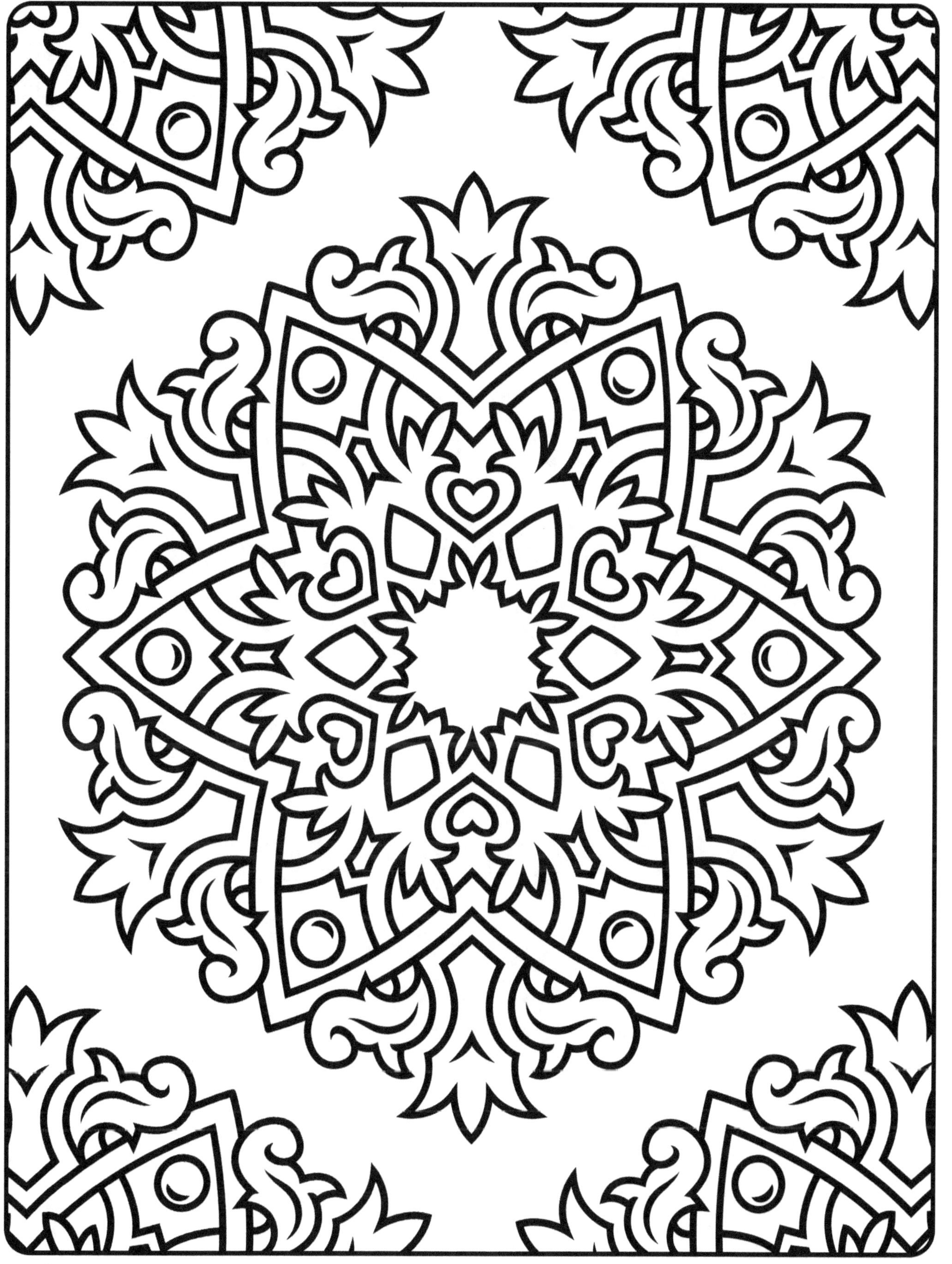

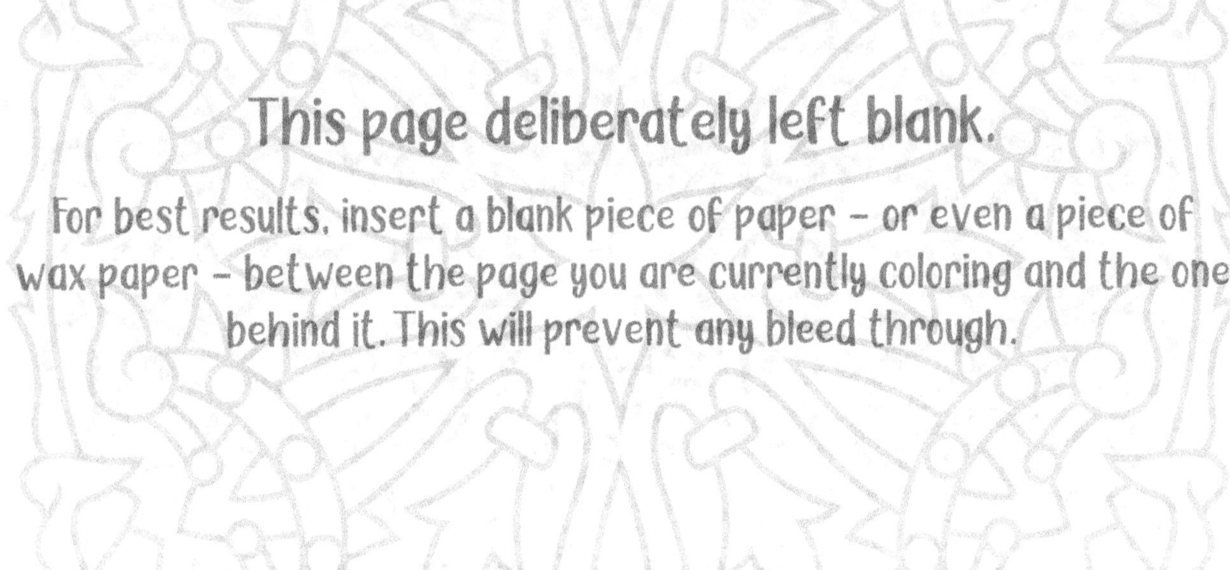

This page deliberately left blank.

For best results, insert a blank piece of paper – or even a piece of wax paper – between the page you are currently coloring and the one behind it. This will prevent any bleed through.

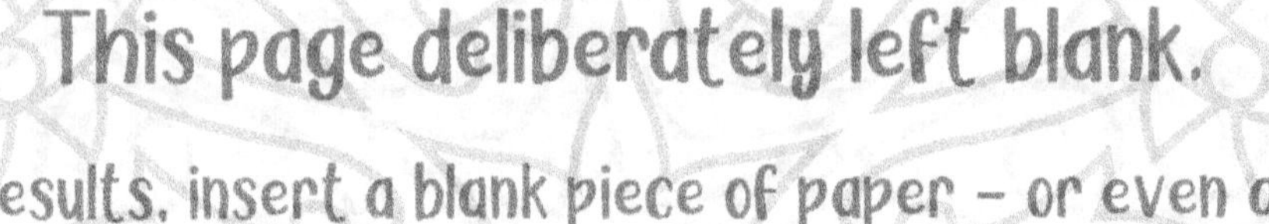

This page deliberately left blank.

For best results, insert a blank piece of paper – or even a piece of wax paper – between the page you are currently coloring and the one behind it. This will prevent any bleed through.

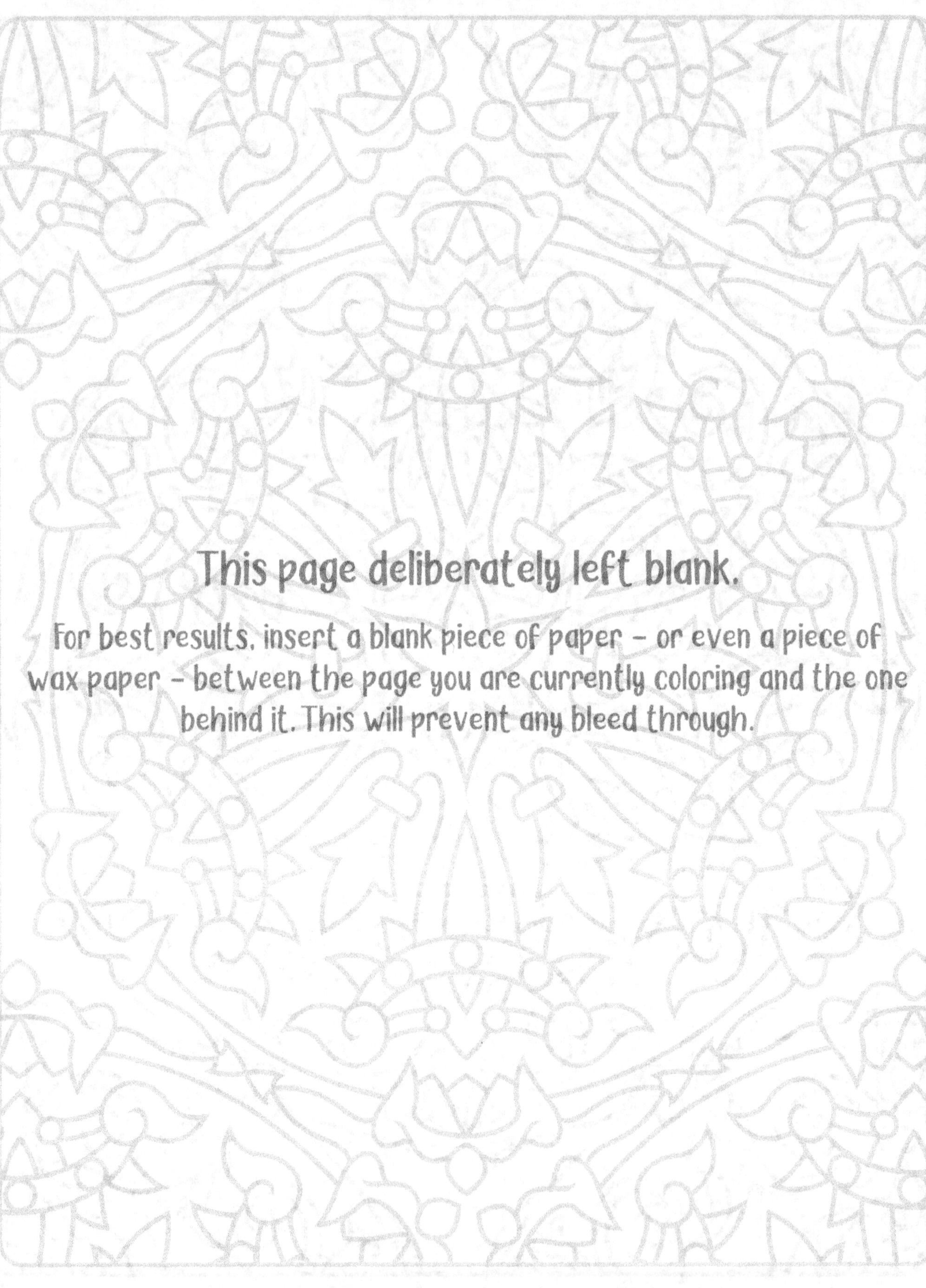

This page deliberately left blank.

For best results, insert a blank piece of paper – or even a piece of wax paper – between the page you are currently coloring and the one behind it. This will prevent any bleed through.

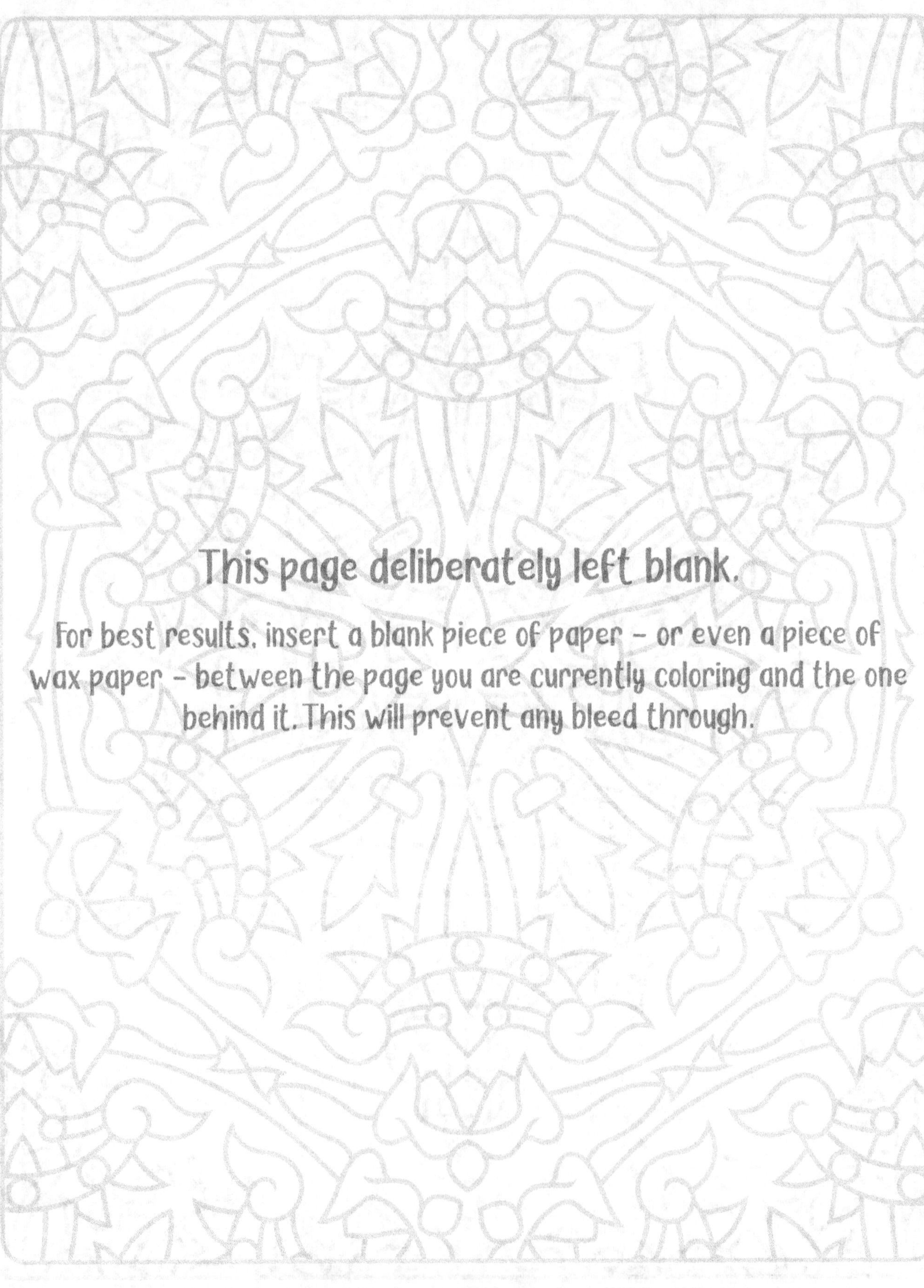

This page deliberately left blank.

For best results, insert a blank piece of paper – or even a piece of wax paper – between the page you are currently coloring and the one behind it. This will prevent any bleed through.

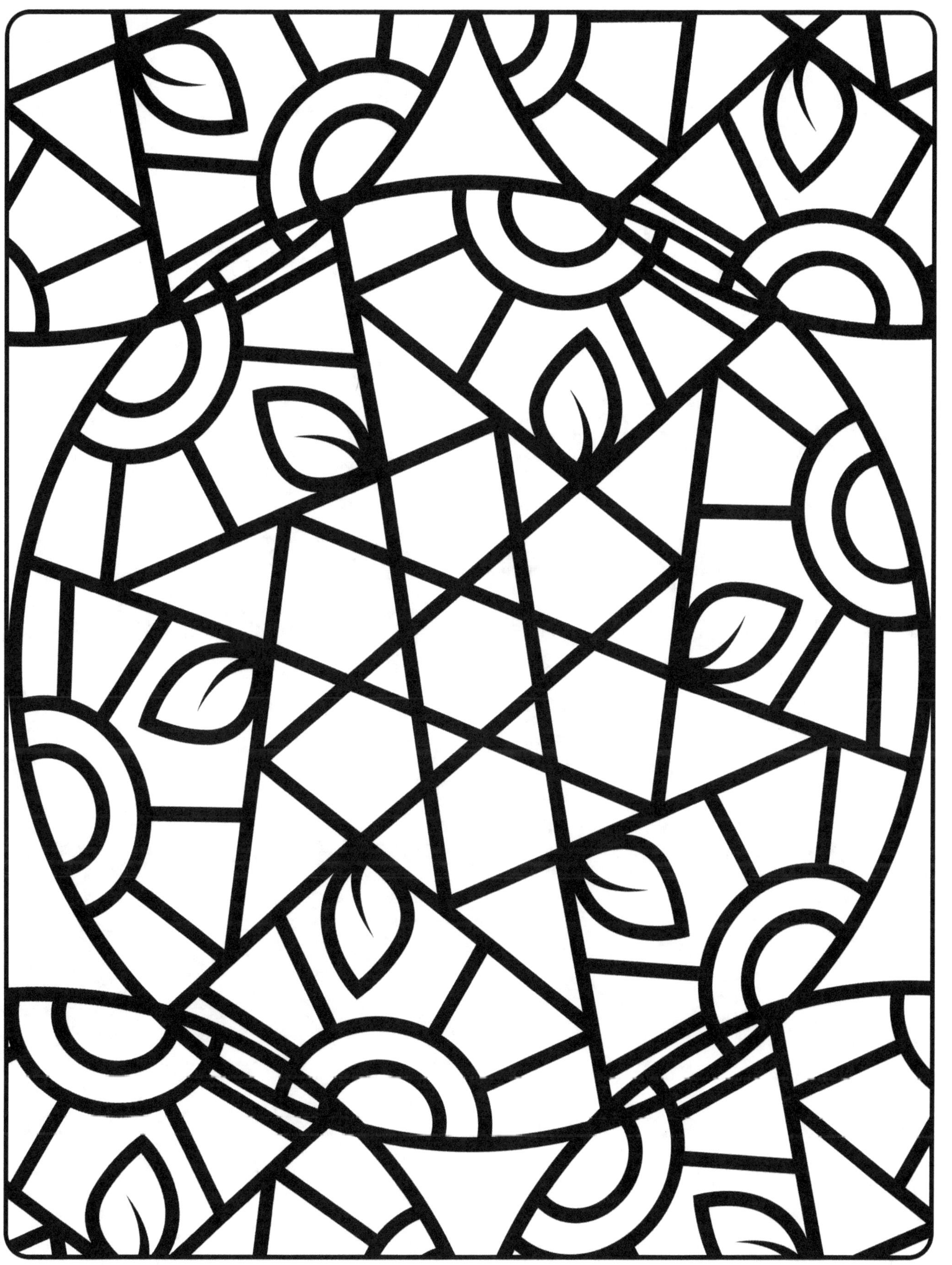

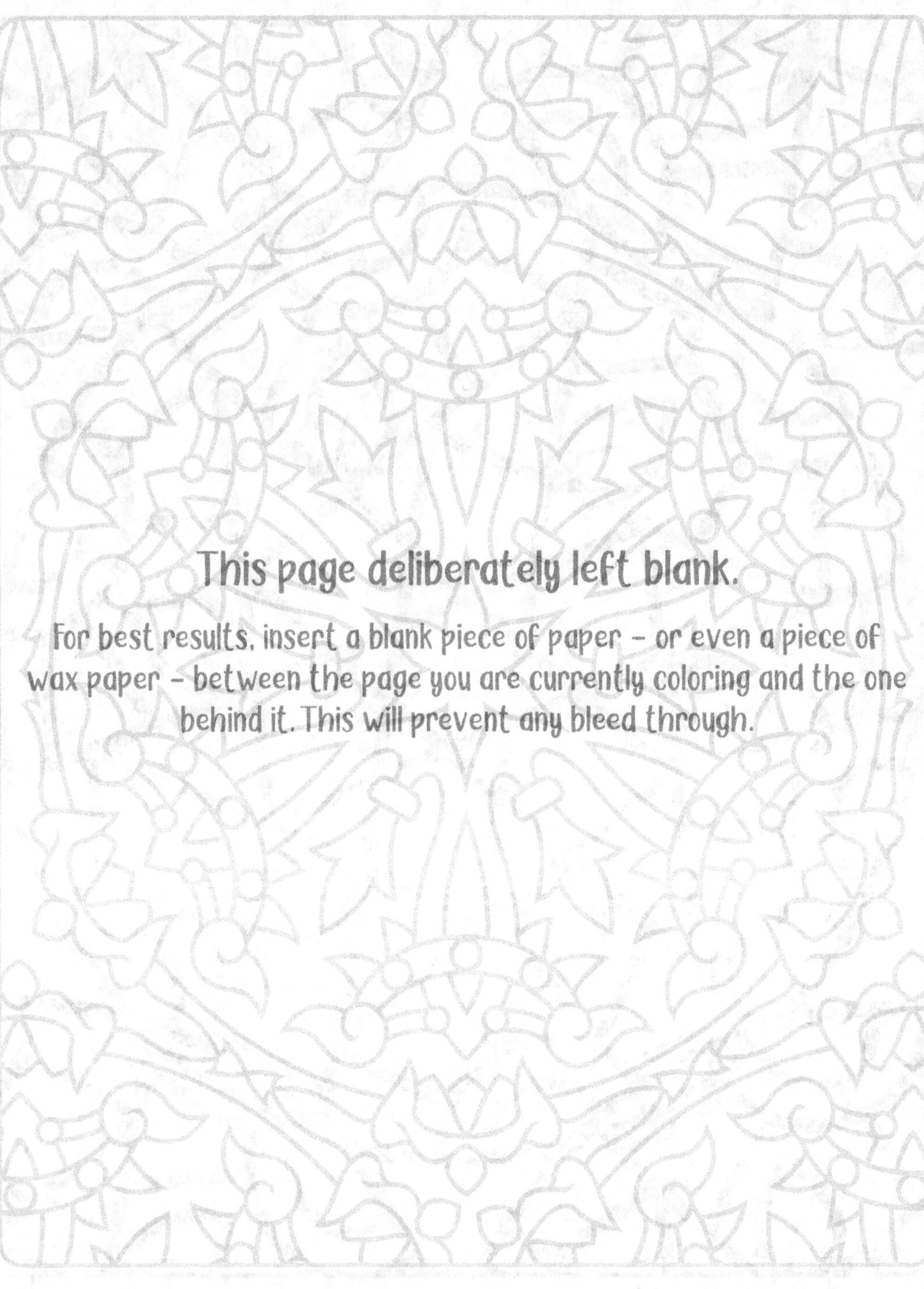

This page deliberately left blank.

For best results, insert a blank piece of paper – or even a piece of wax paper – between the page you are currently coloring and the one behind it. This will prevent any bleed through.

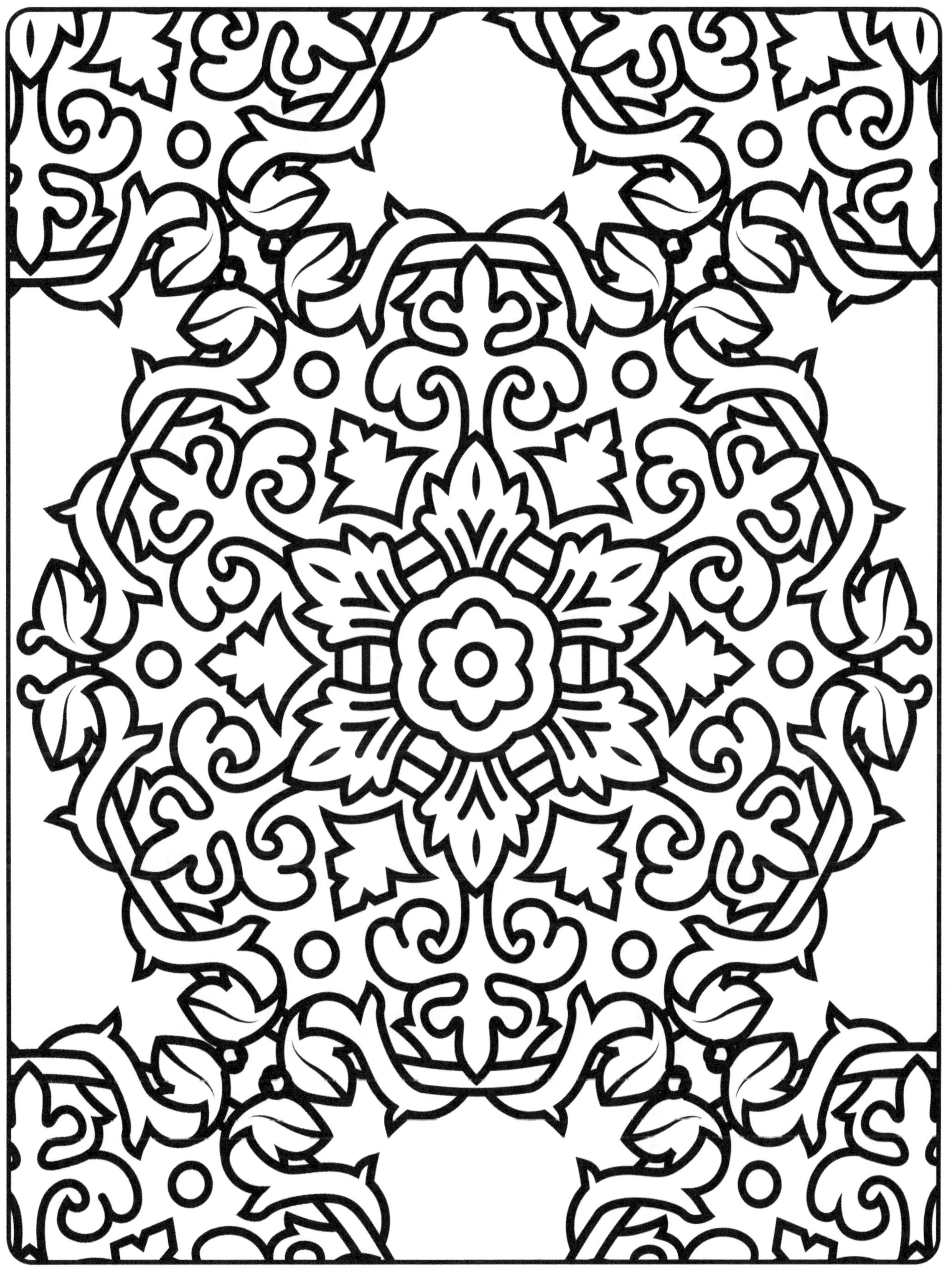

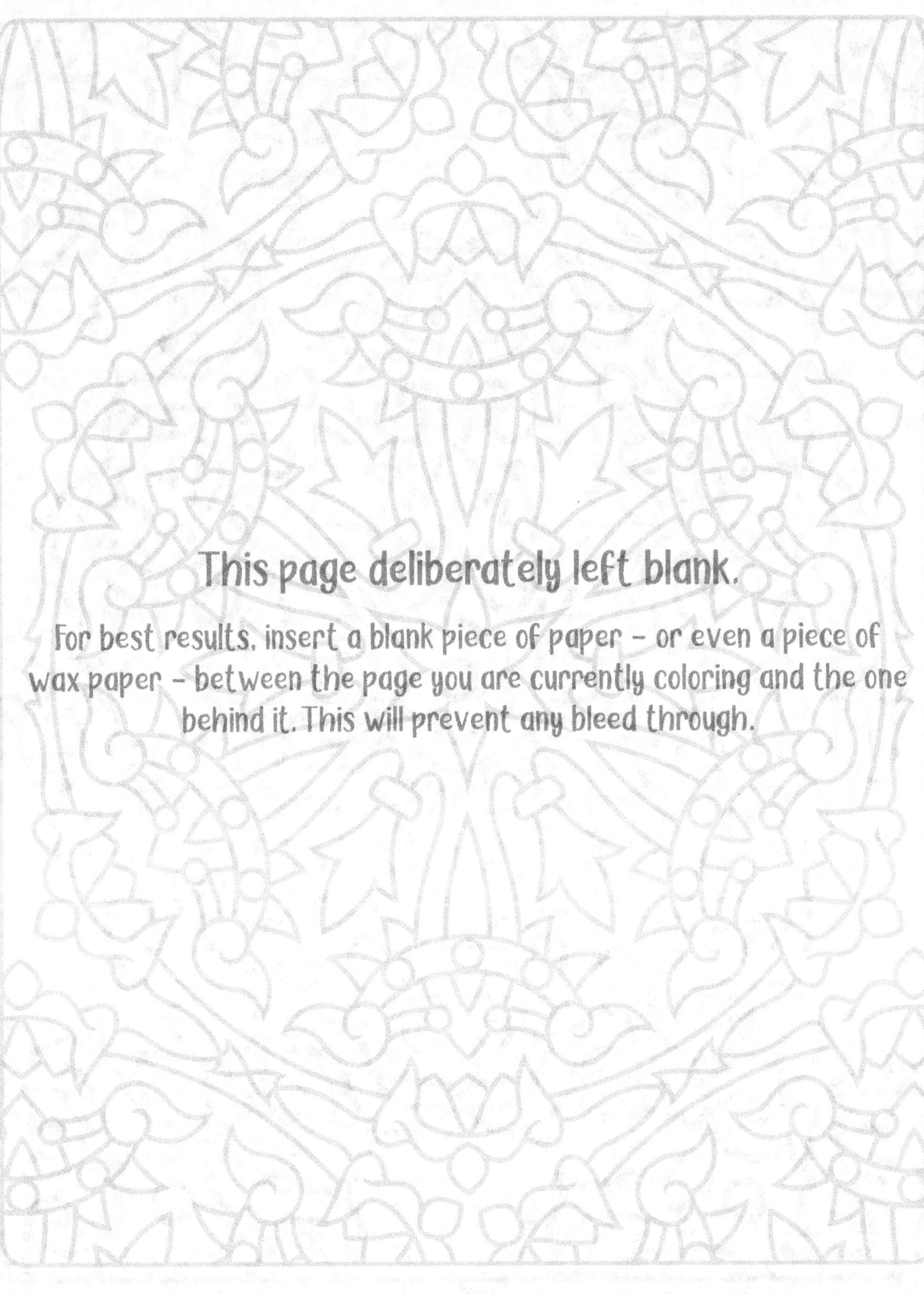

This page deliberately left blank.

For best results, insert a blank piece of paper – or even a piece of wax paper – between the page you are currently coloring and the one behind it. This will prevent any bleed through.

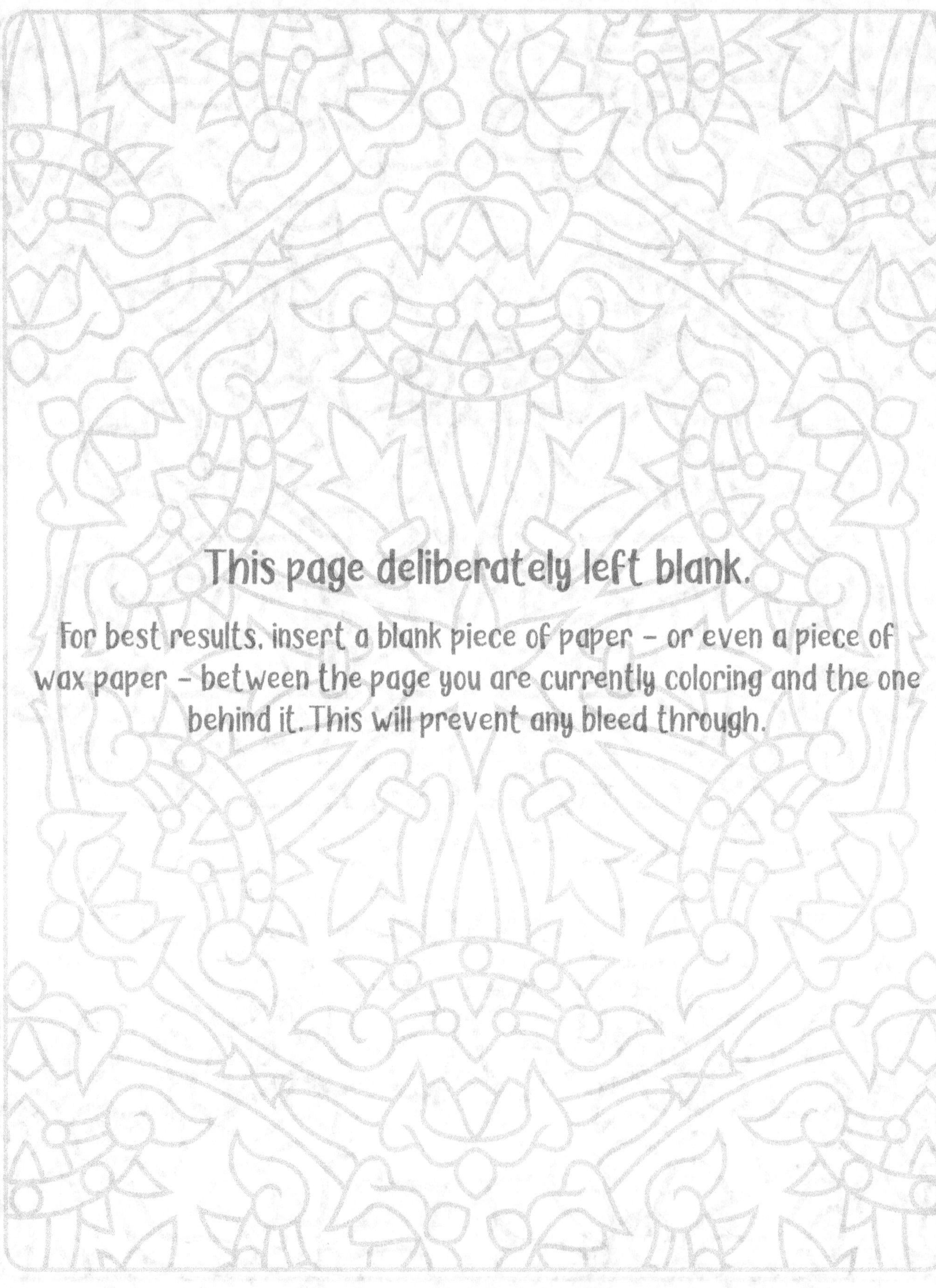

This page deliberately left blank.

For best results, insert a blank piece of paper – or even a piece of wax paper – between the page you are currently coloring and the one behind it. This will prevent any bleed through.

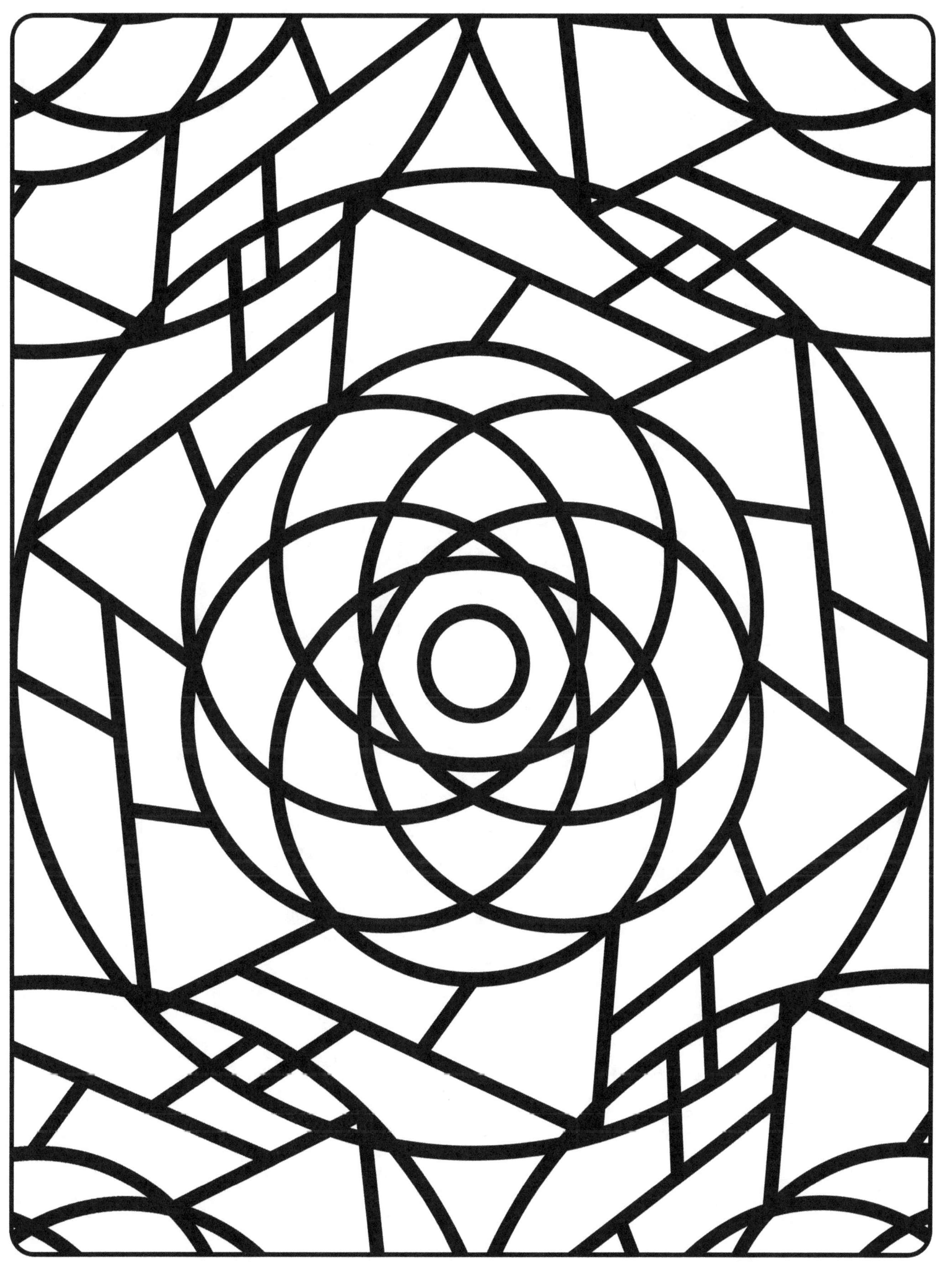

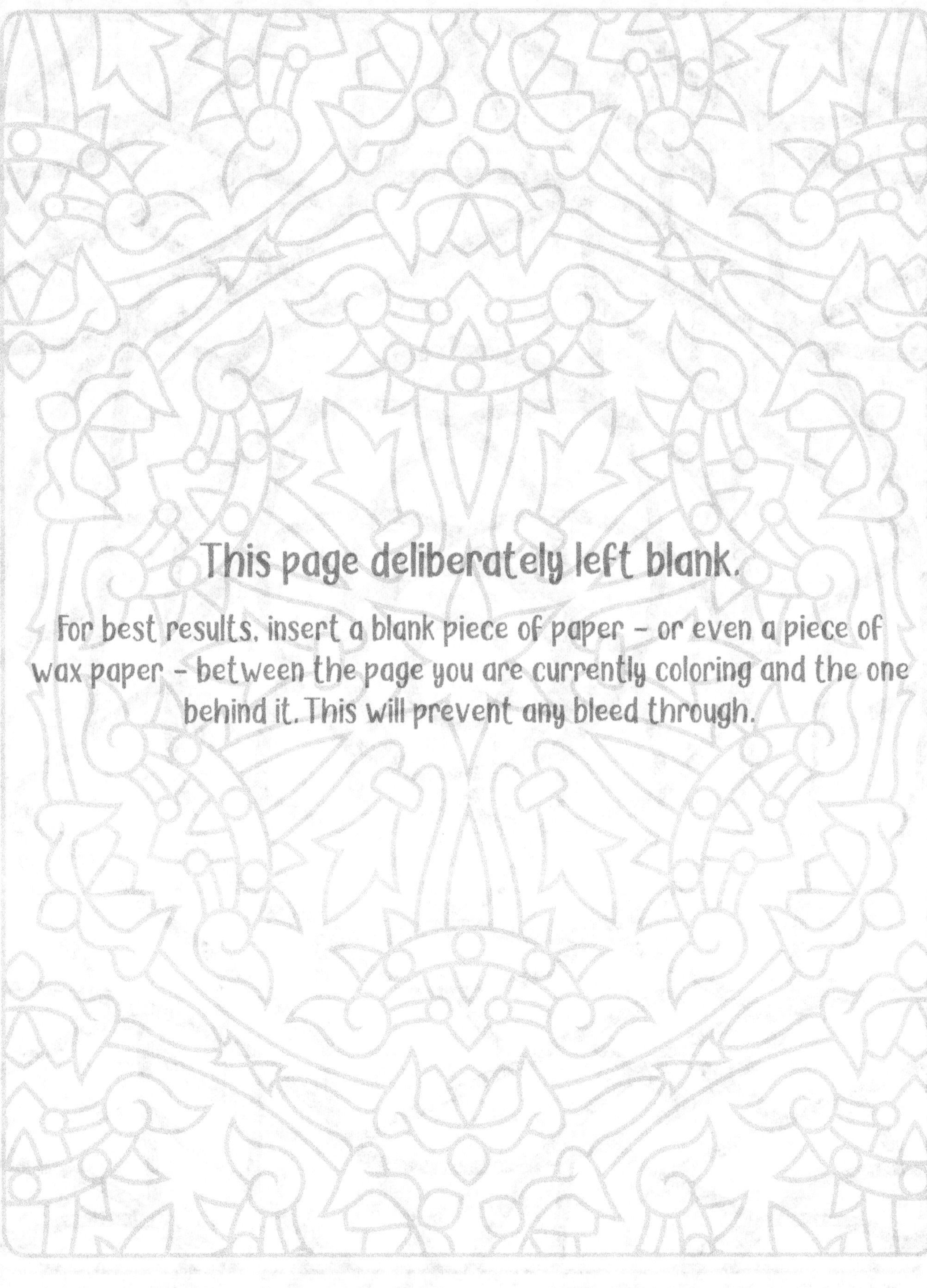

This page deliberately left blank.

For best results, insert a blank piece of paper – or even a piece of wax paper – between the page you are currently coloring and the one behind it. This will prevent any bleed through.

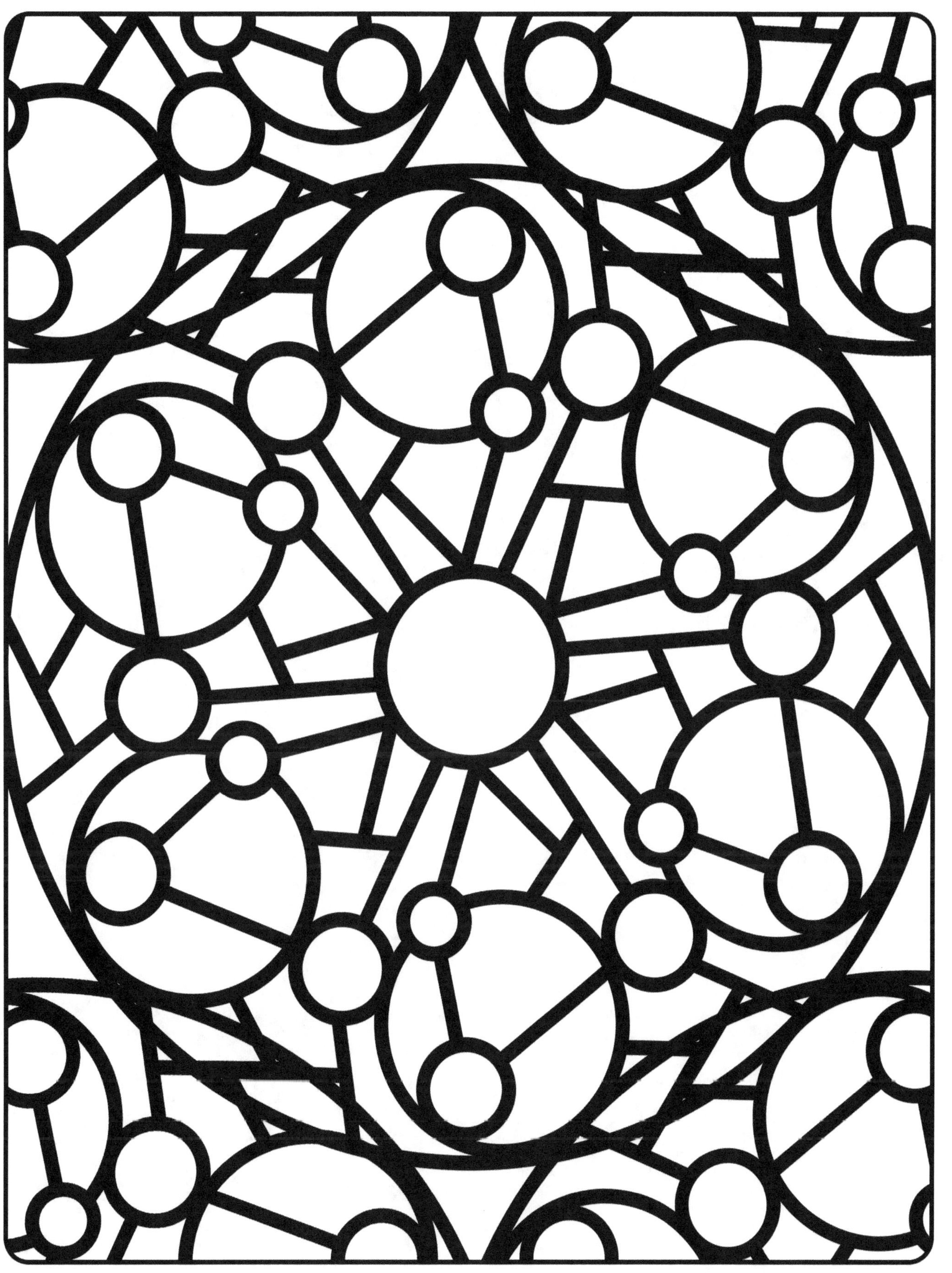

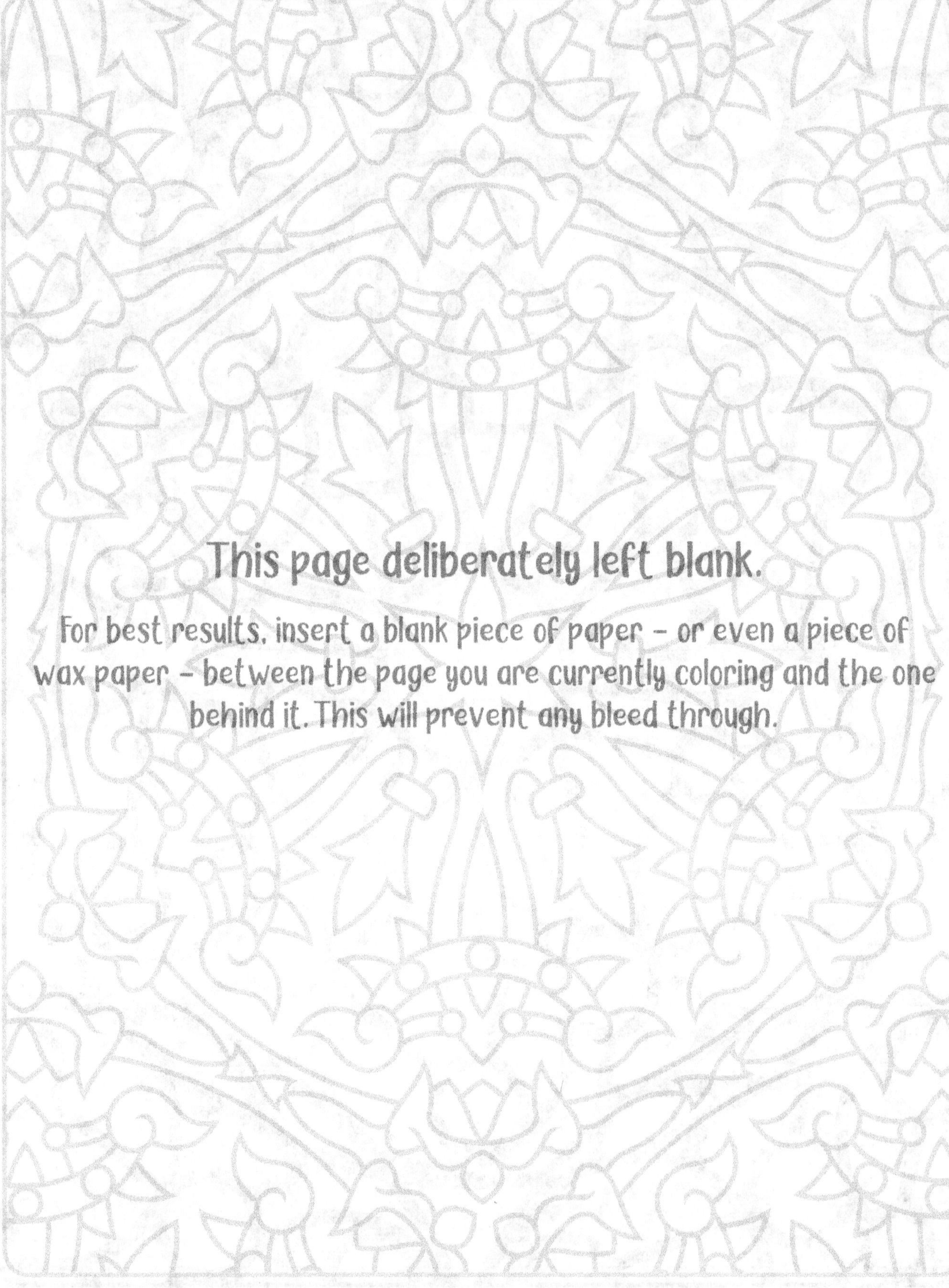

This page deliberately left blank.

For best results, insert a blank piece of paper – or even a piece of wax paper – between the page you are currently coloring and the one behind it. This will prevent any bleed through.

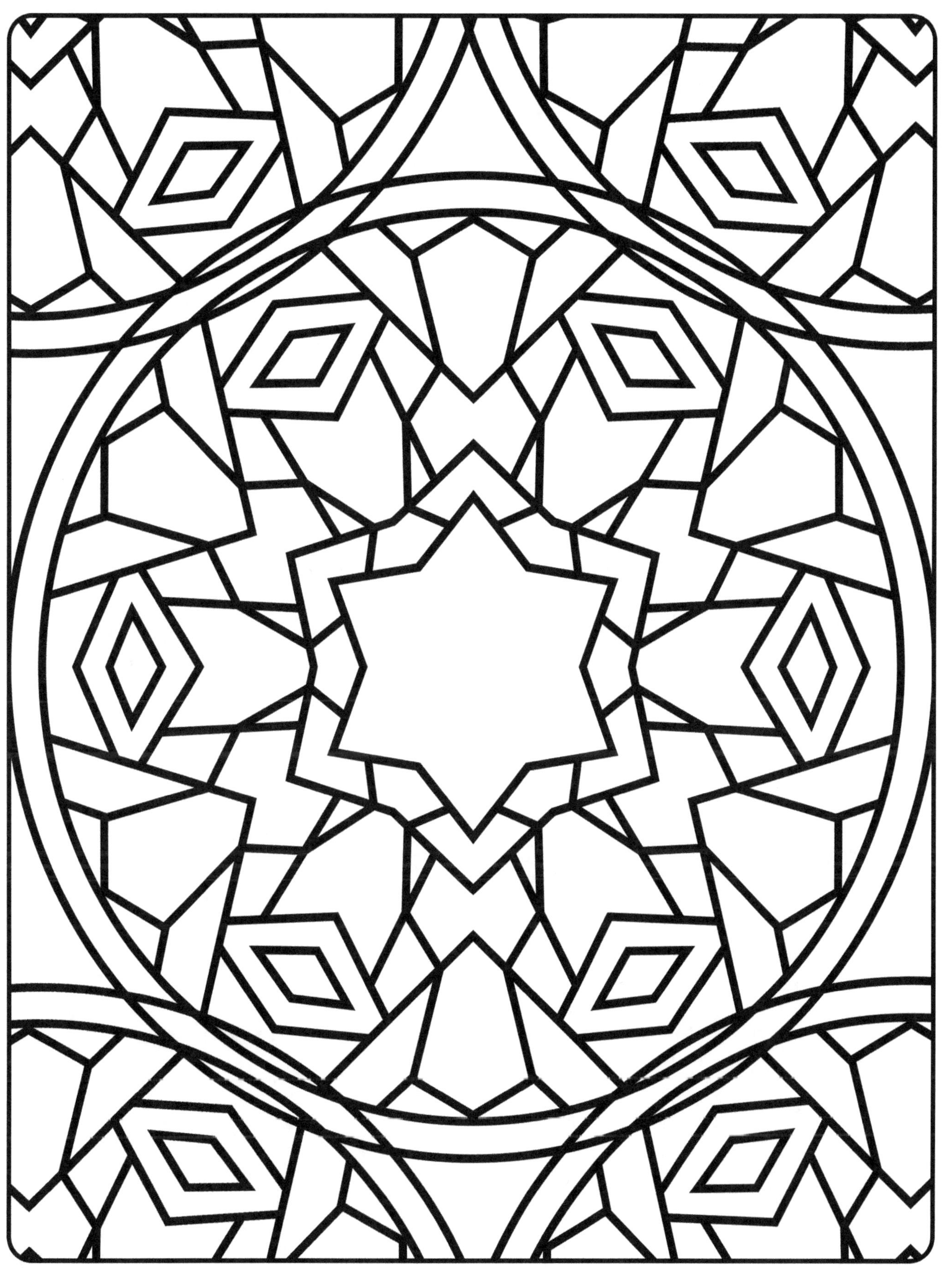

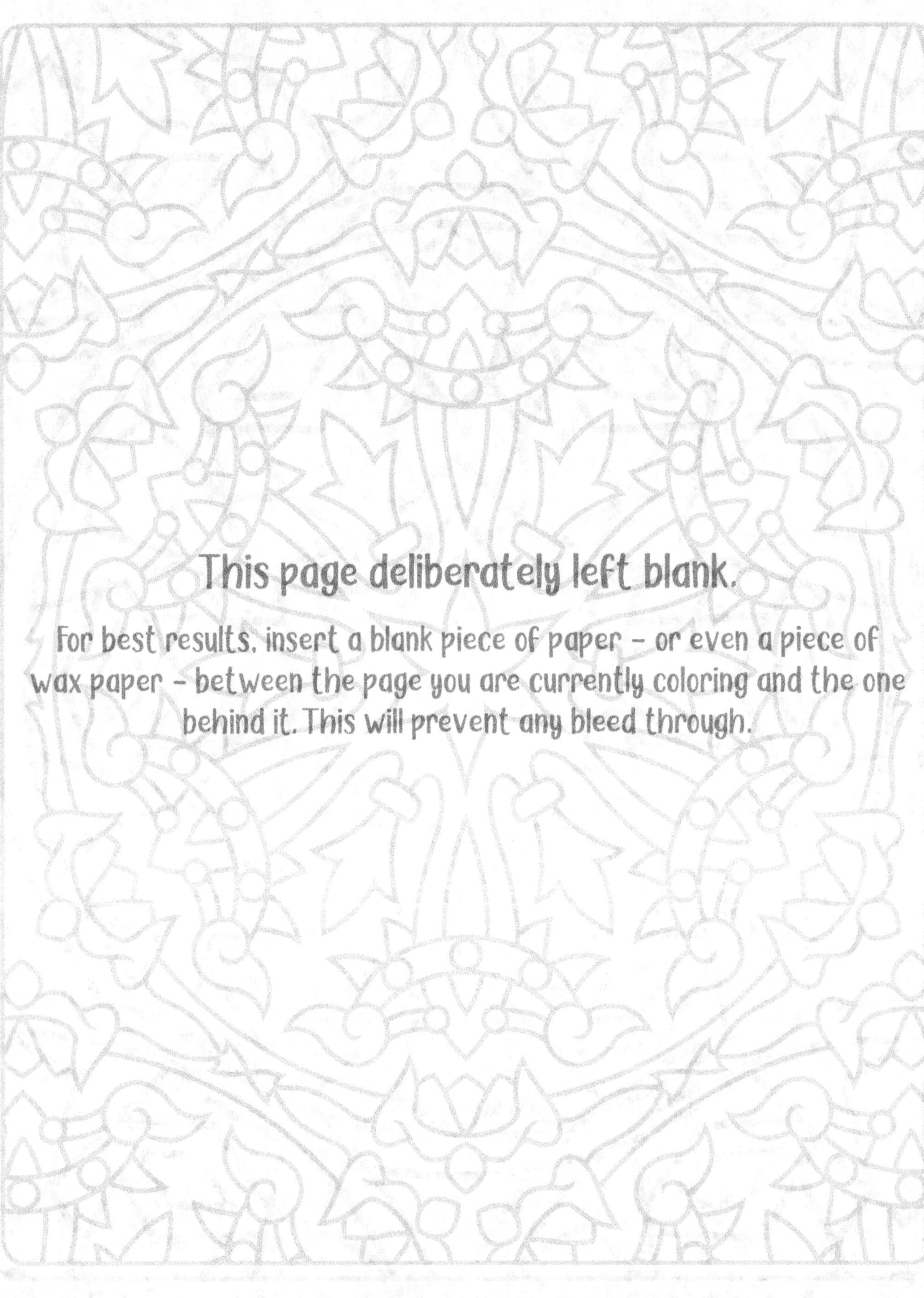

This page deliberately left blank.

For best results, insert a blank piece of paper – or even a piece of wax paper – between the page you are currently coloring and the one behind it. This will prevent any bleed through.

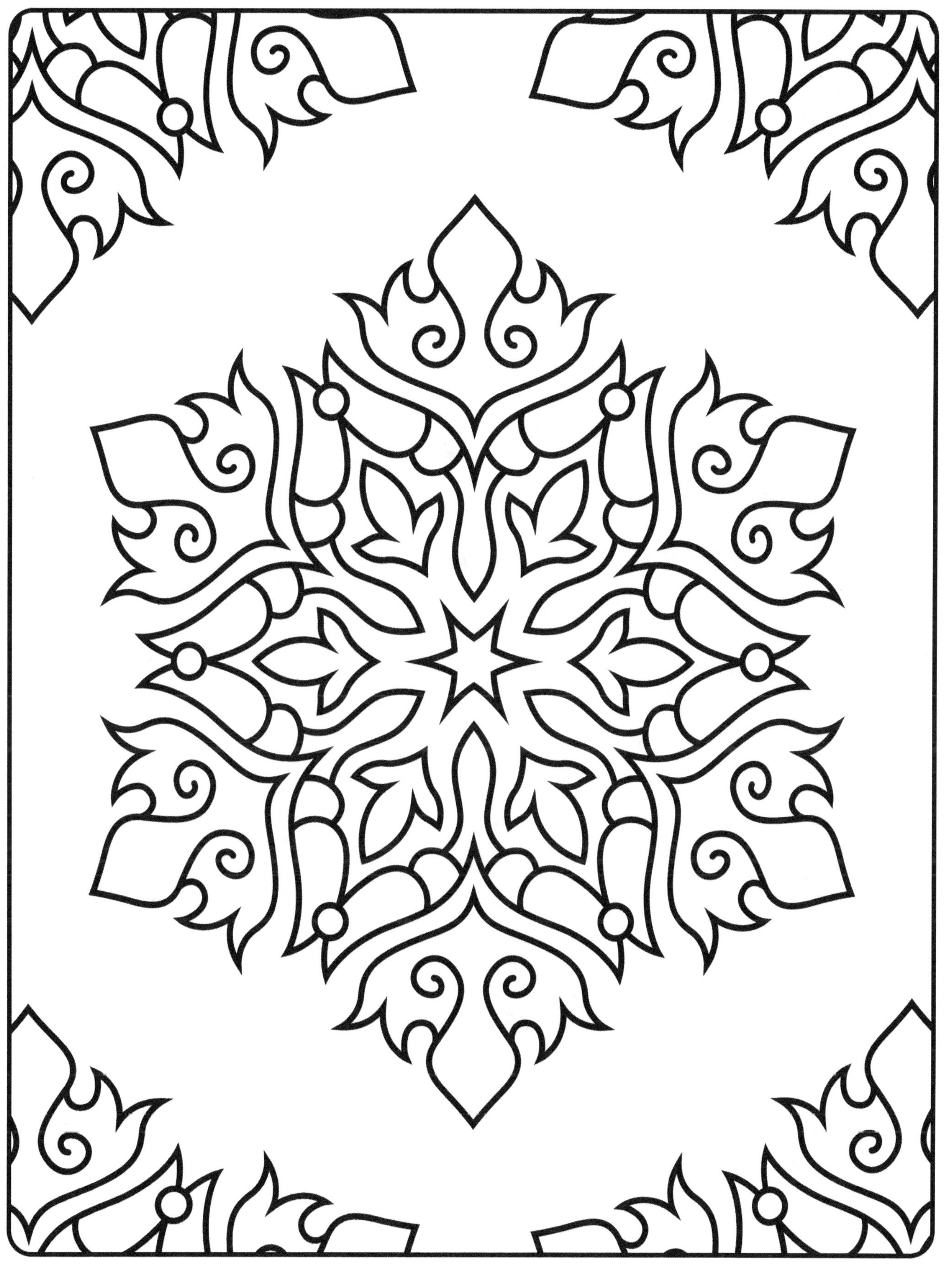

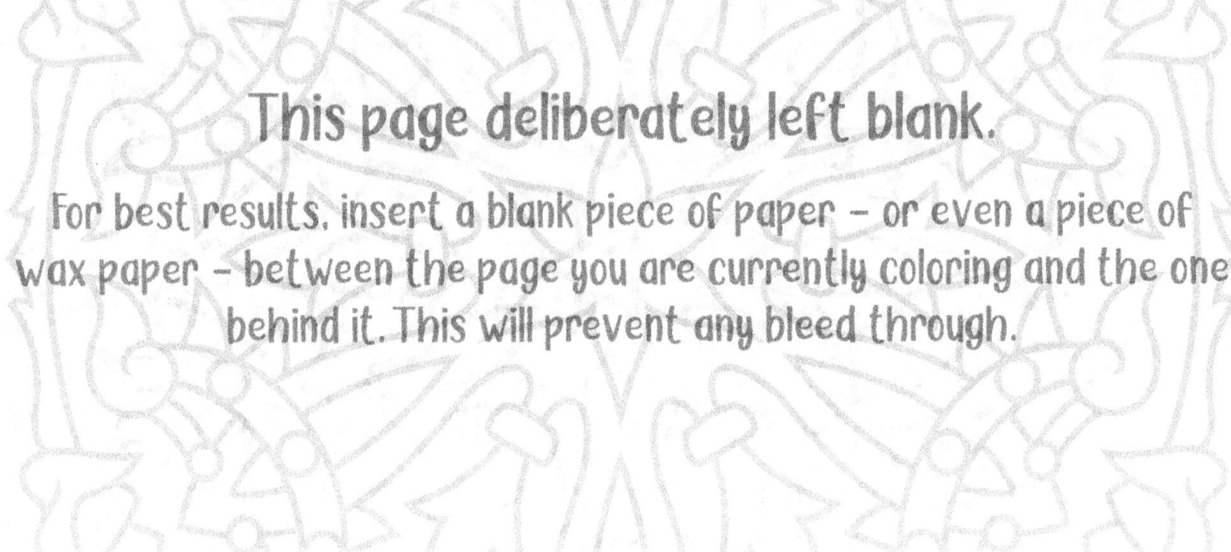

This page deliberately left blank.

For best results, insert a blank piece of paper – or even a piece of wax paper – between the page you are currently coloring and the one behind it. This will prevent any bleed through.

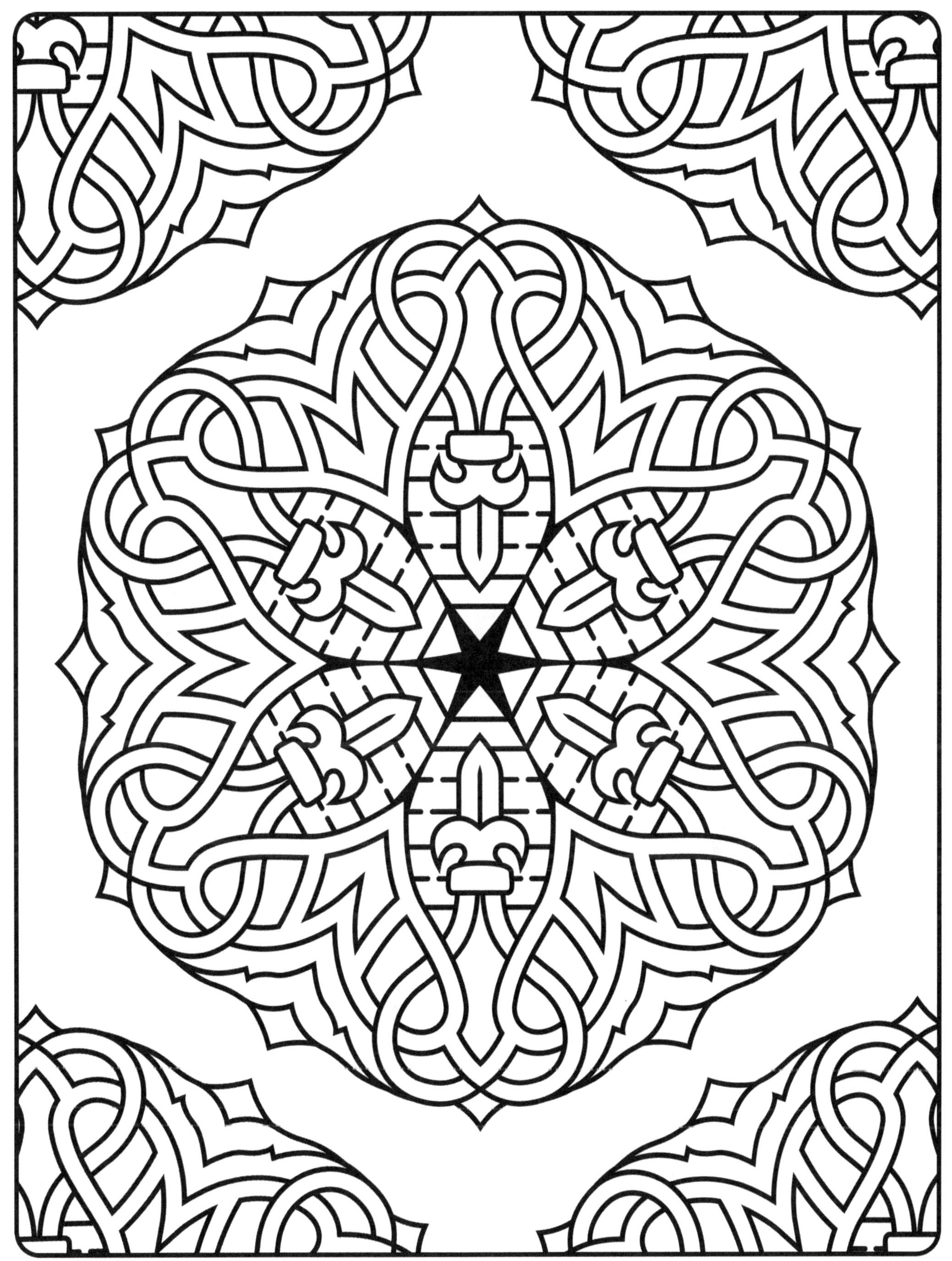

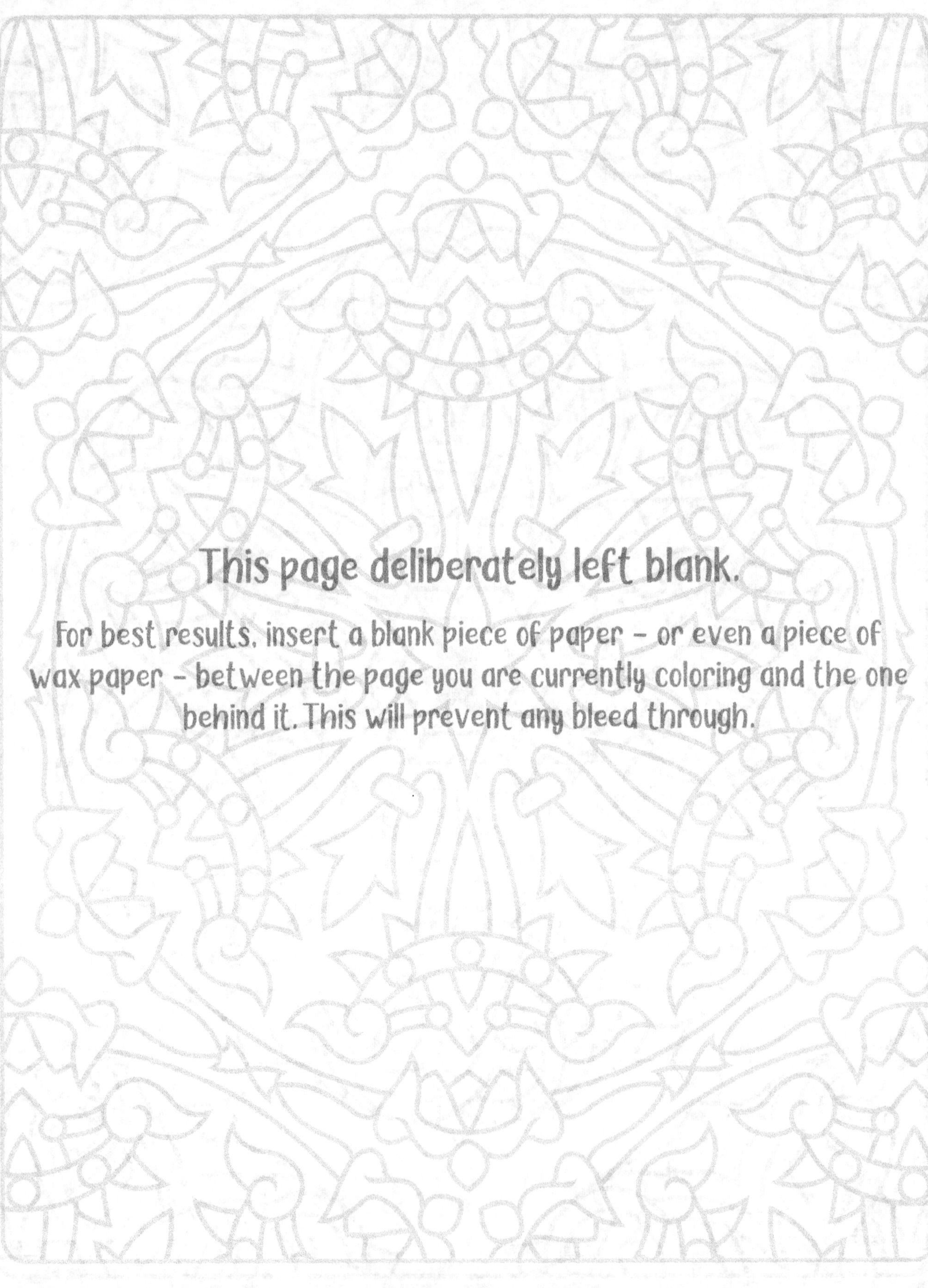

This page deliberately left blank.

For best results, insert a blank piece of paper – or even a piece of wax paper – between the page you are currently coloring and the one behind it. This will prevent any bleed through.

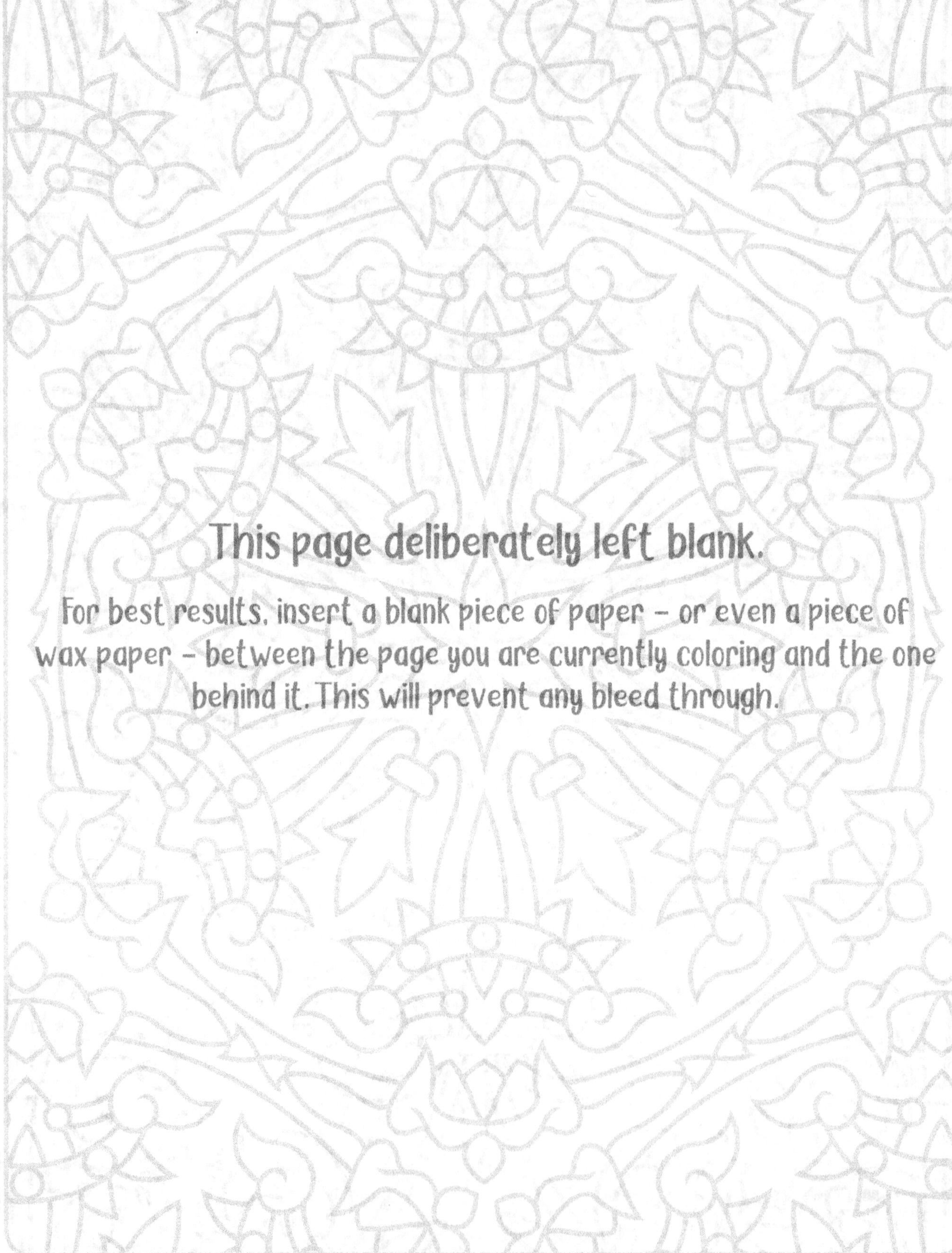

This page deliberately left blank.

For best results, insert a blank piece of paper – or even a piece of wax paper – between the page you are currently coloring and the one behind it. This will prevent any bleed through.

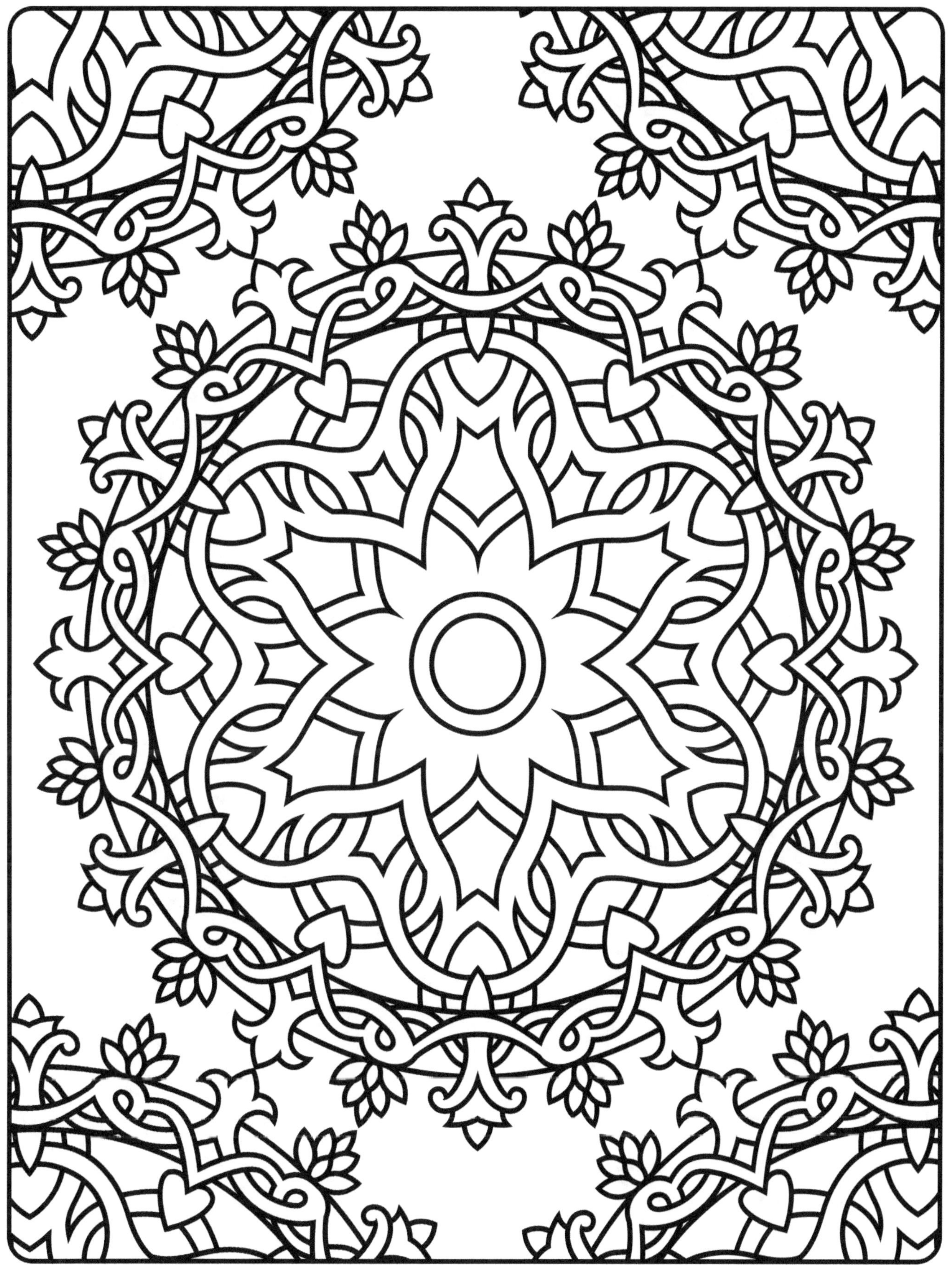

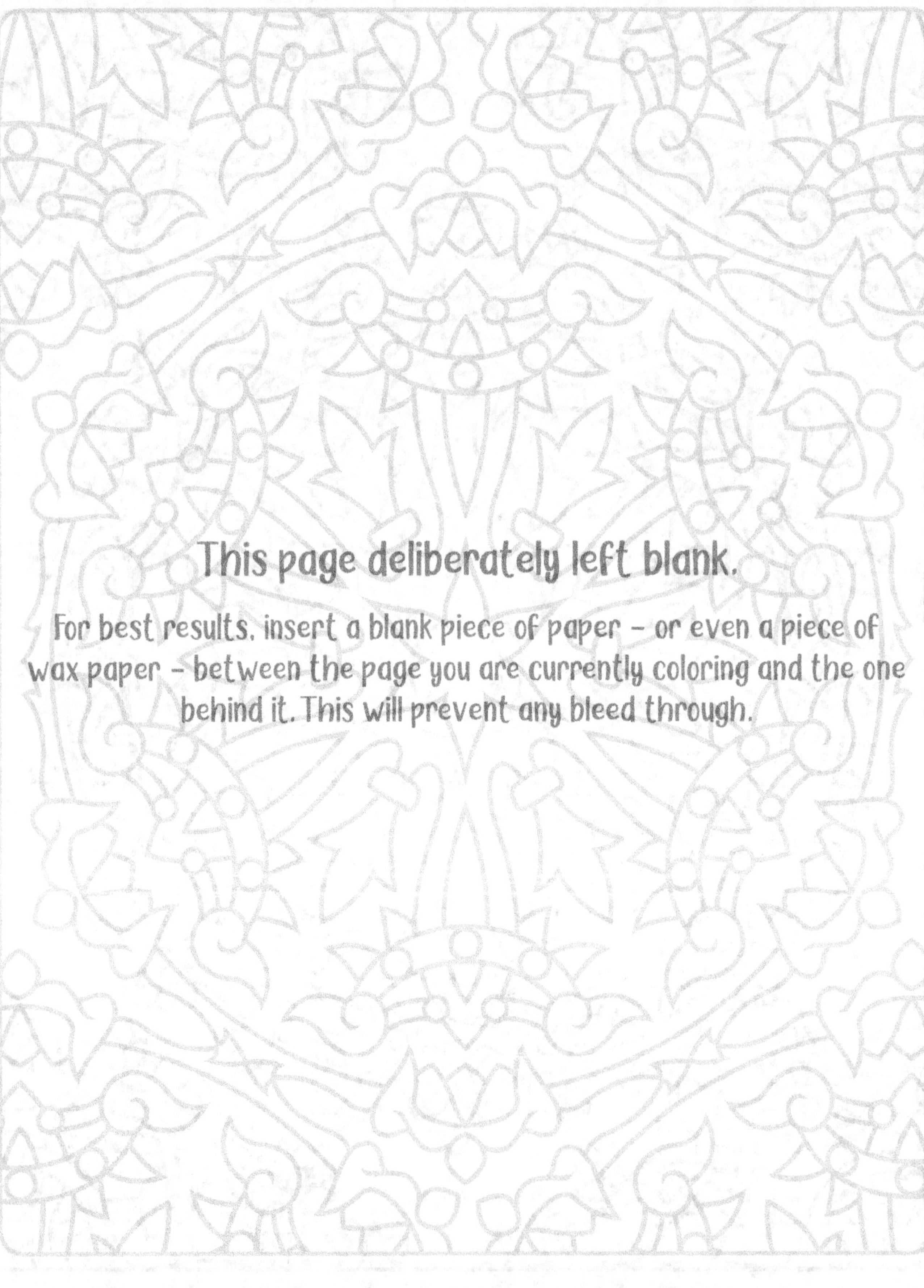

This page deliberately left blank.

For best results, insert a blank piece of paper - or even a piece of wax paper - between the page you are currently coloring and the one behind it. This will prevent any bleed through.

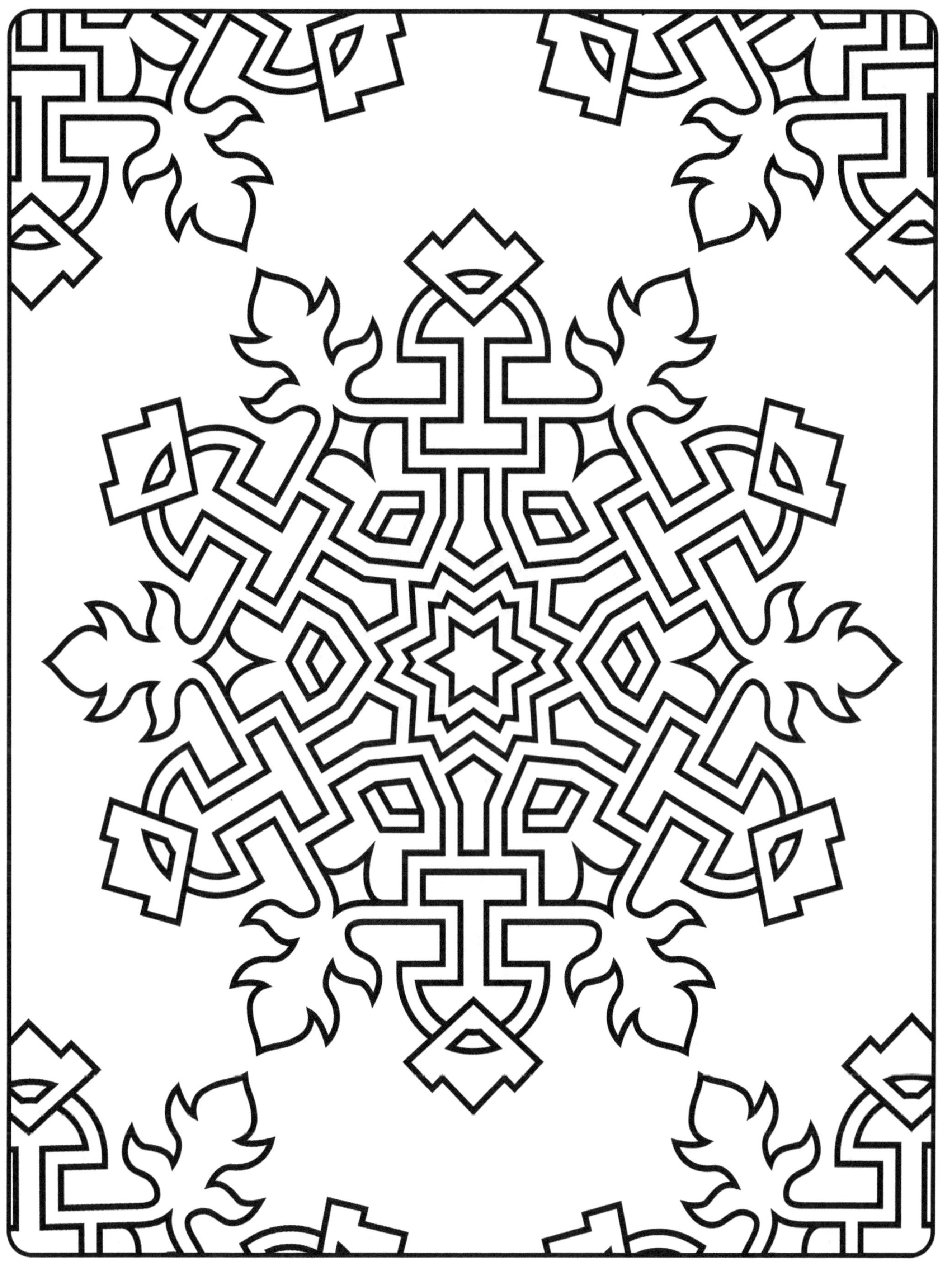

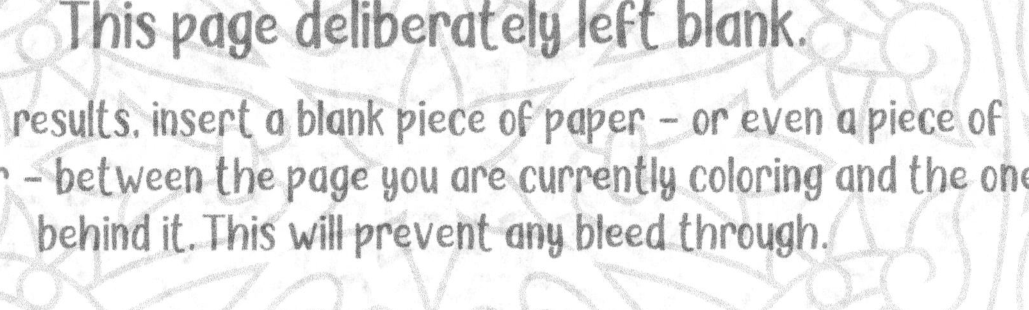

This page deliberately left blank.

For best results, insert a blank piece of paper - or even a piece of wax paper - between the page you are currently coloring and the one behind it. This will prevent any bleed through.

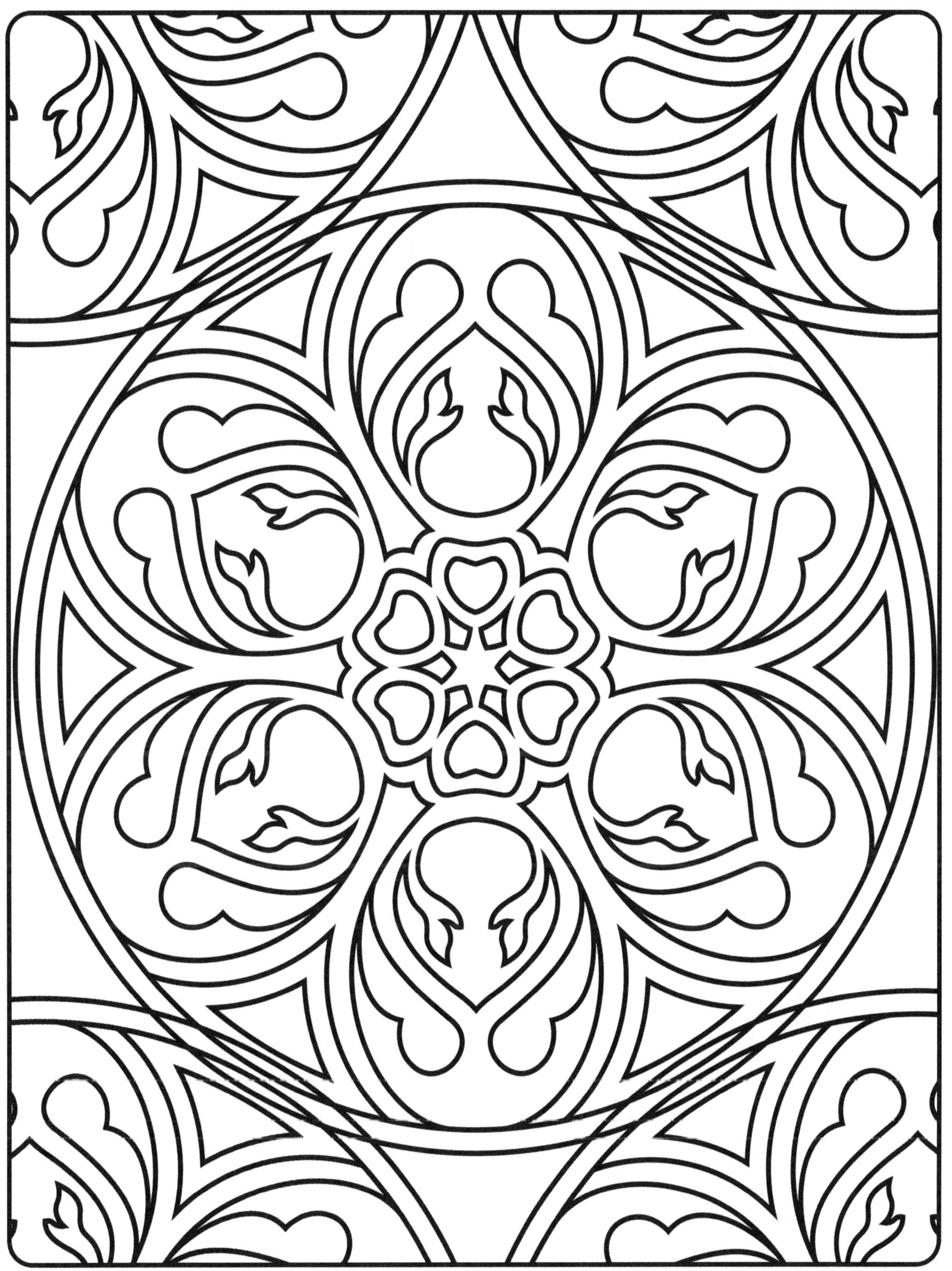

This page deliberately left blank.

For best results, insert a blank piece of paper – or even a piece of wax paper – between the page you are currently coloring and the one behind it. This will prevent any bleed through.

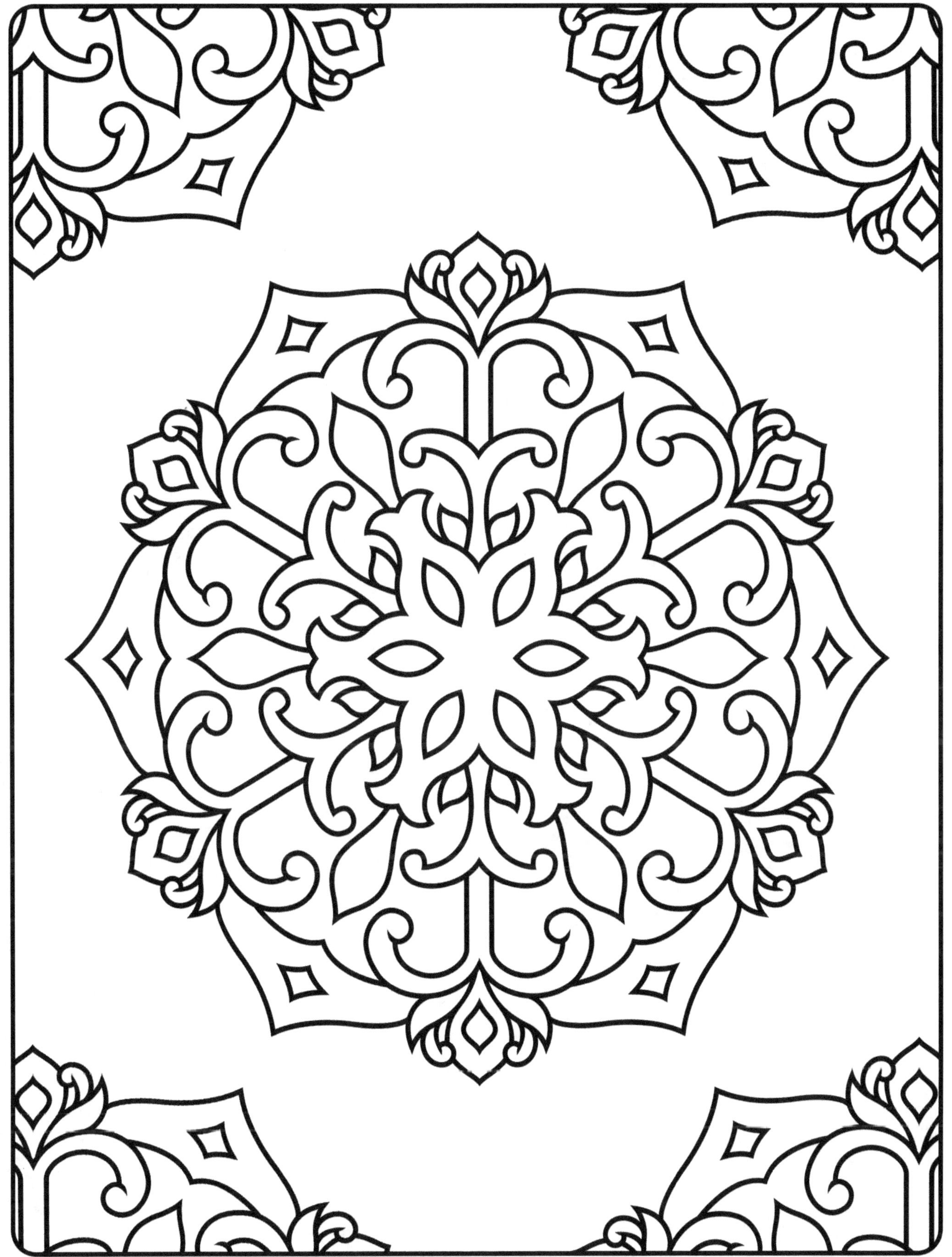

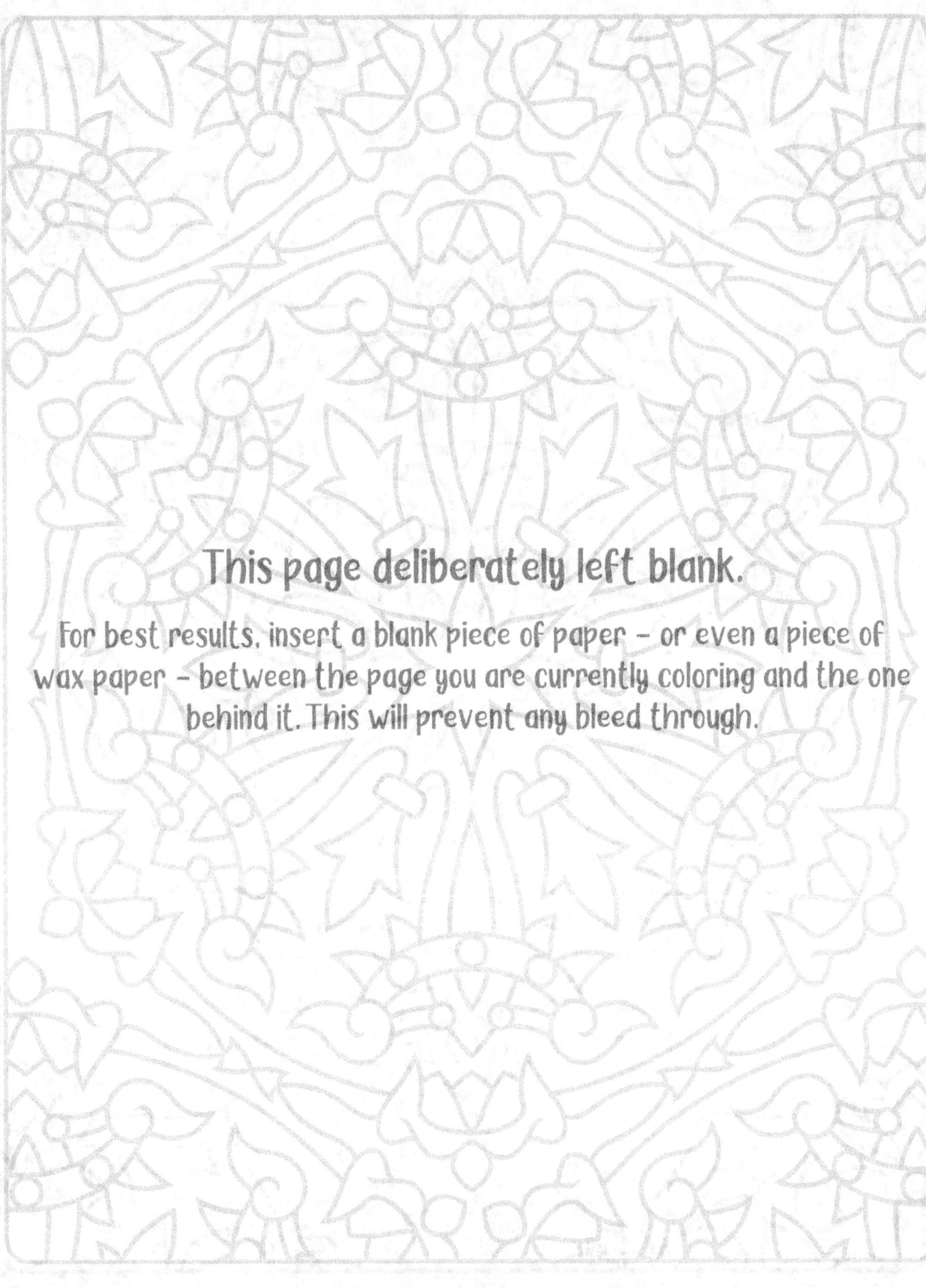

This page deliberately left blank.

For best results, insert a blank piece of paper – or even a piece of wax paper – between the page you are currently coloring and the one behind it. This will prevent any bleed through.

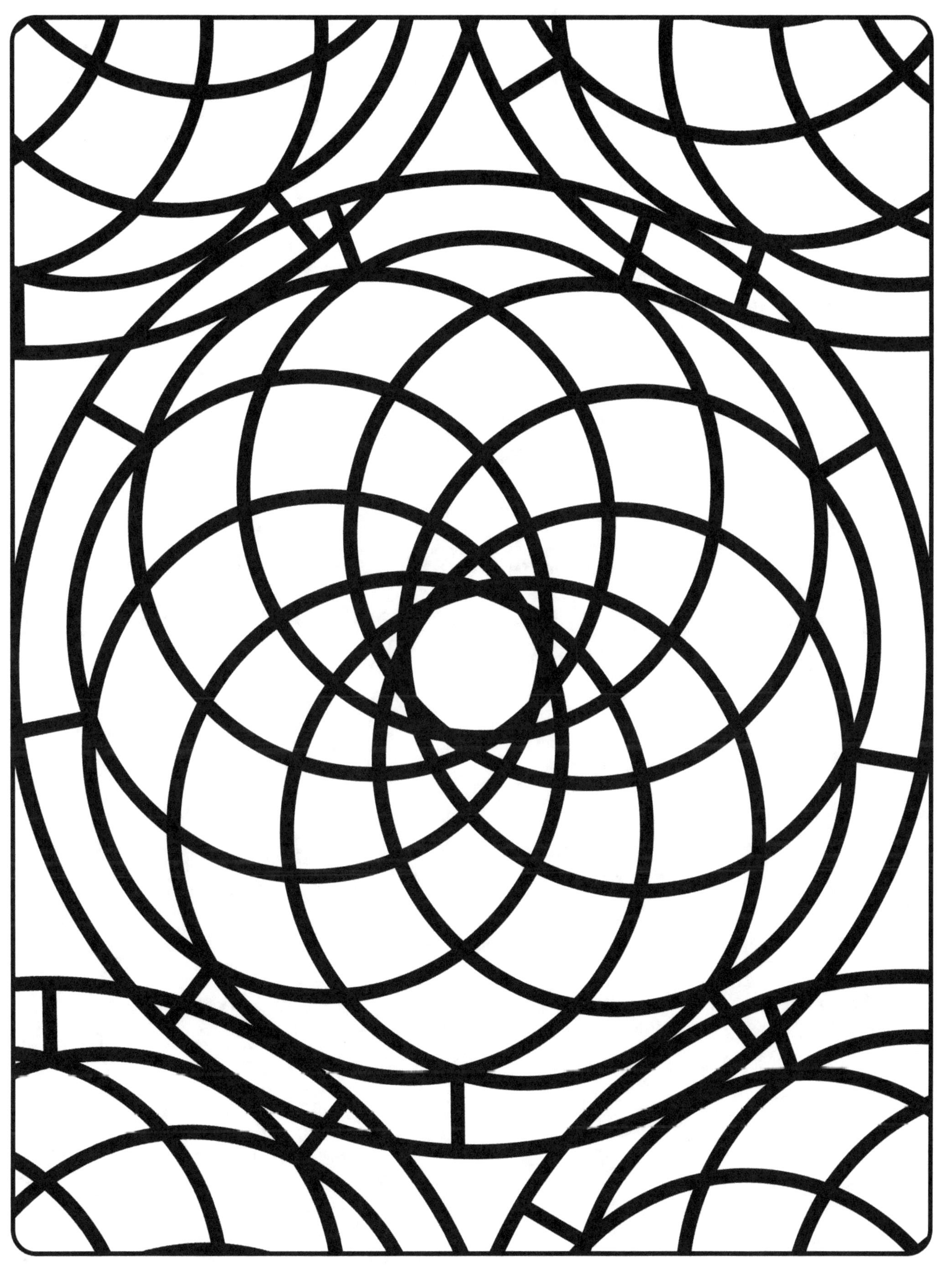

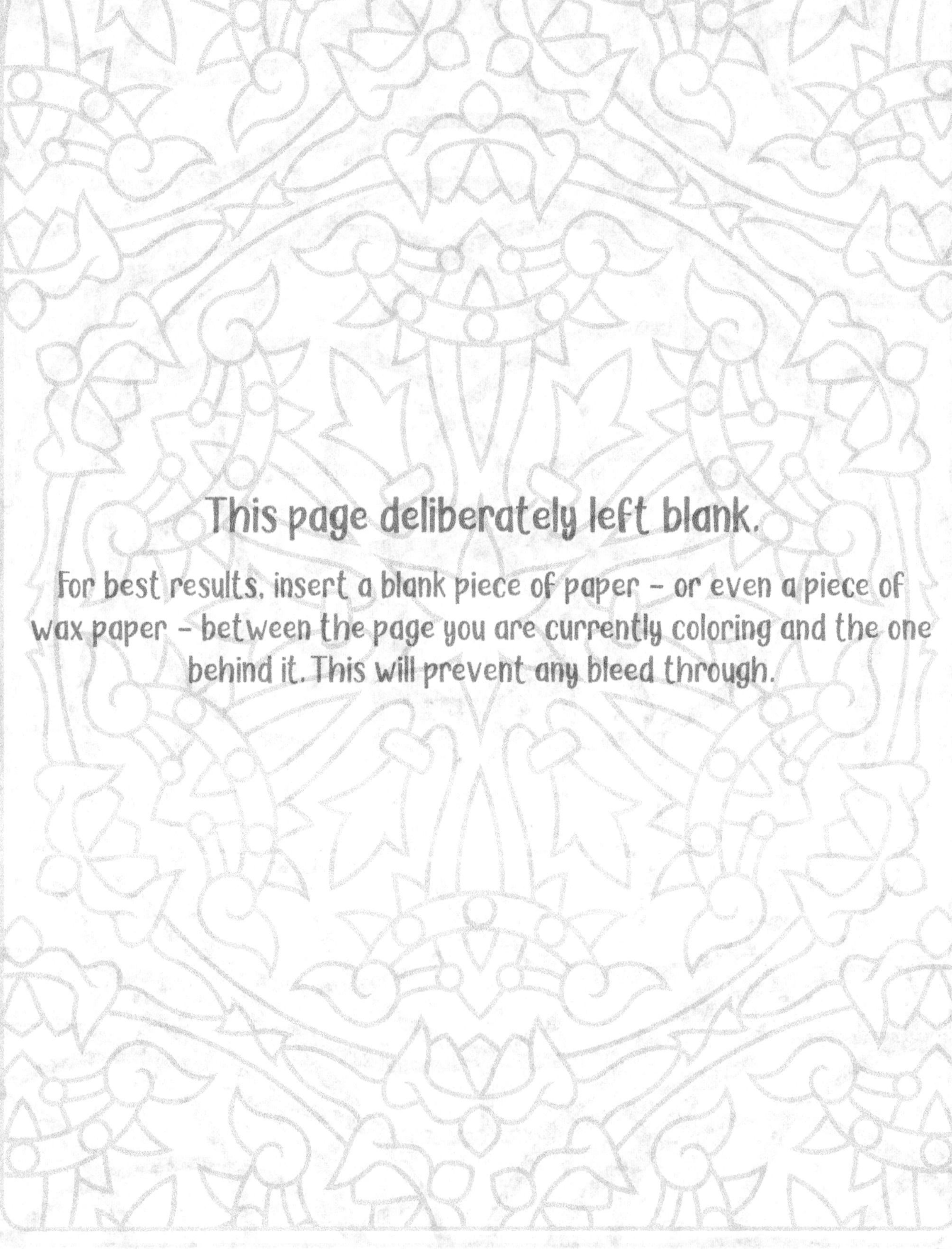

This page deliberately left blank.

For best results, insert a blank piece of paper – or even a piece of wax paper – between the page you are currently coloring and the one behind it. This will prevent any bleed through.

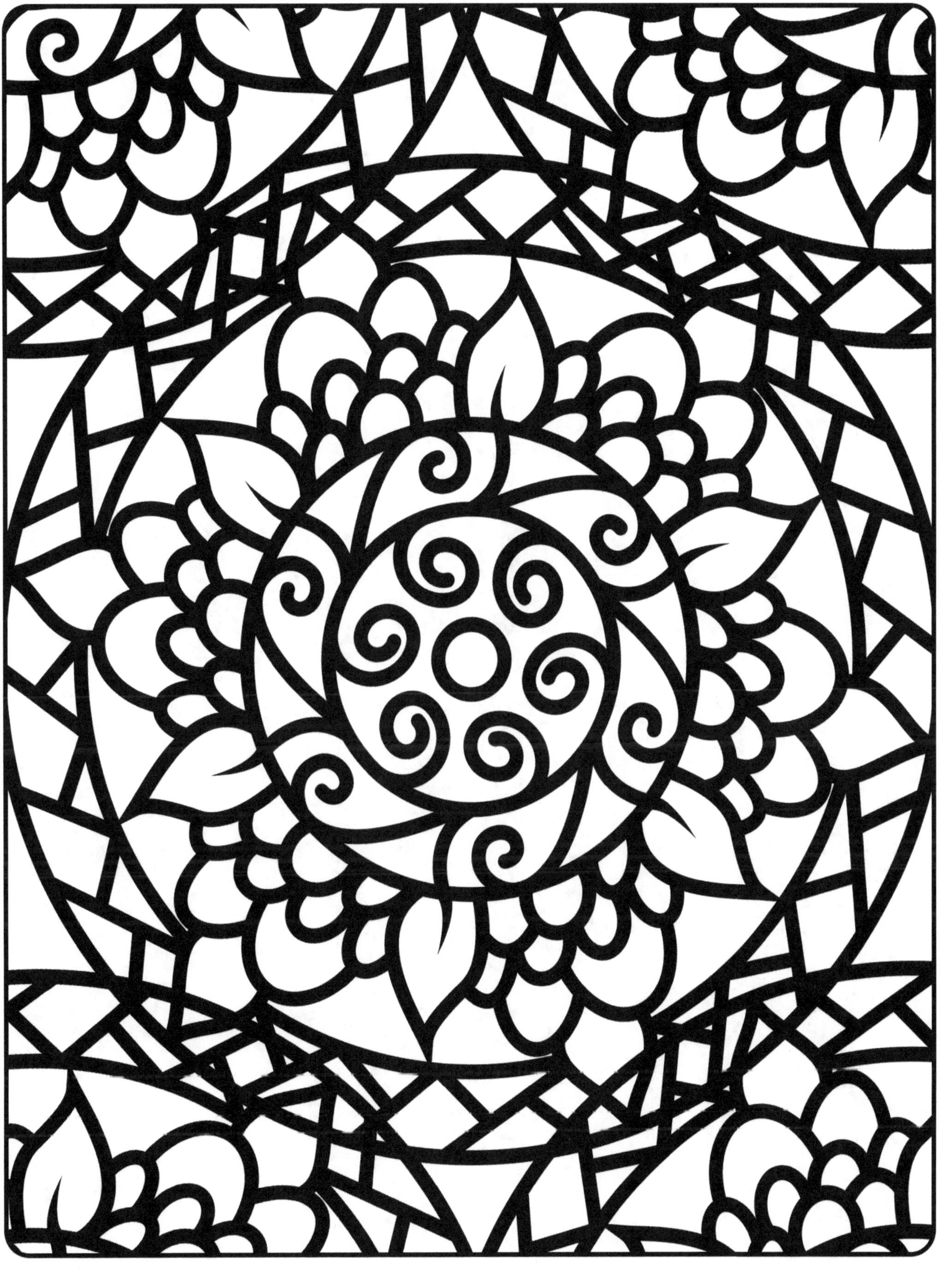

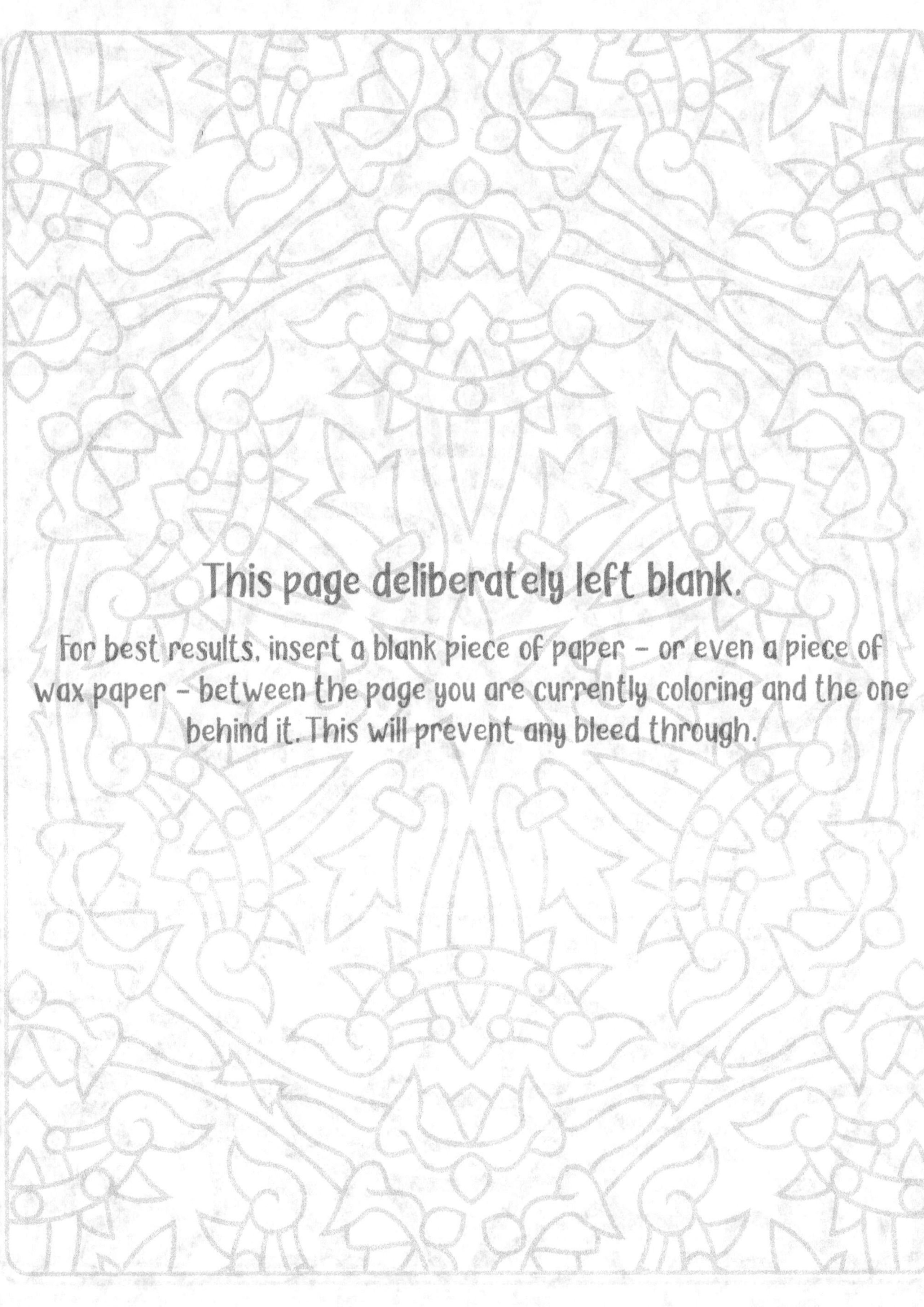
This page deliberately left blank.
For best results, insert a blank piece of paper – or even a piece of wax paper – between the page you are currently coloring and the one behind it. This will prevent any bleed through.

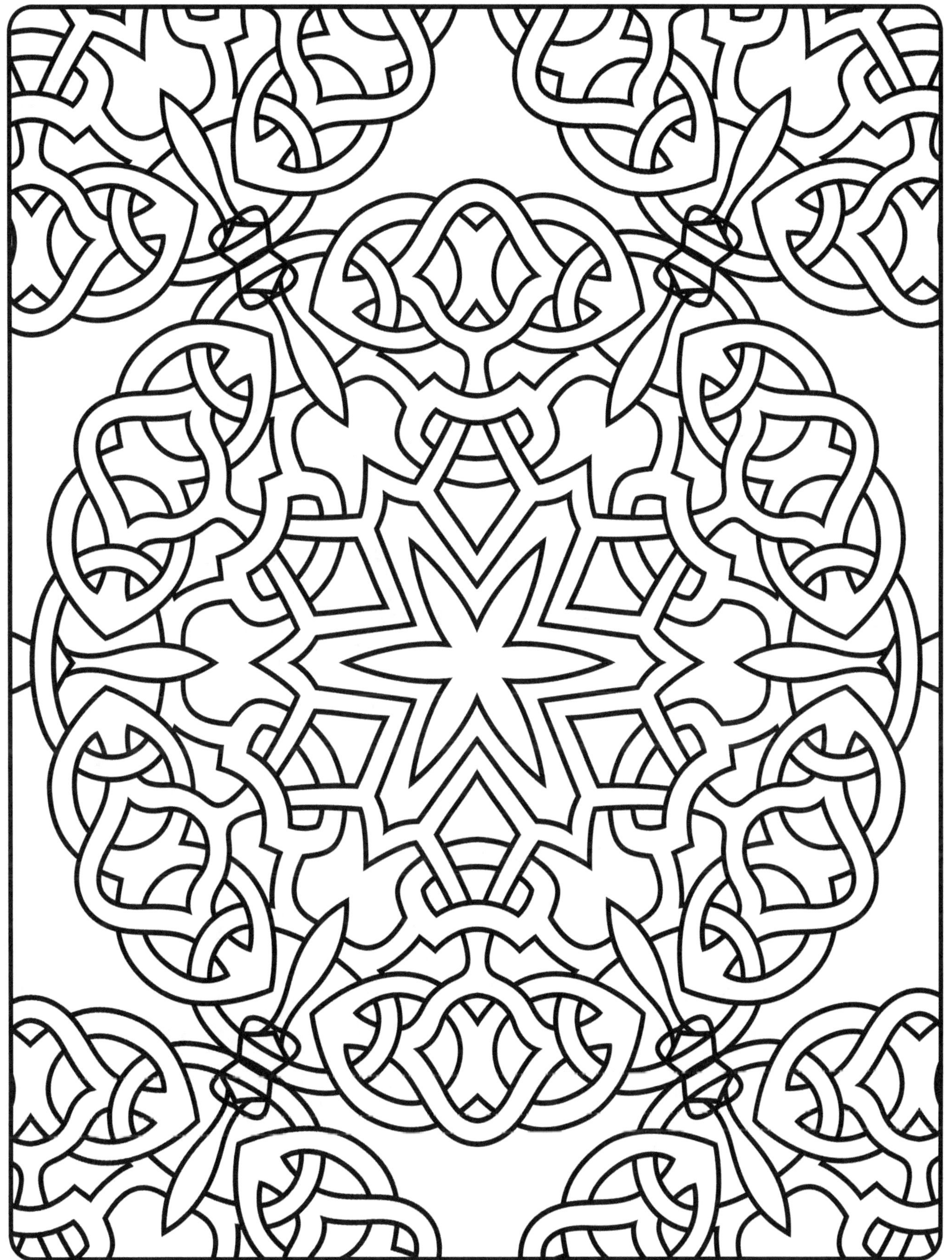

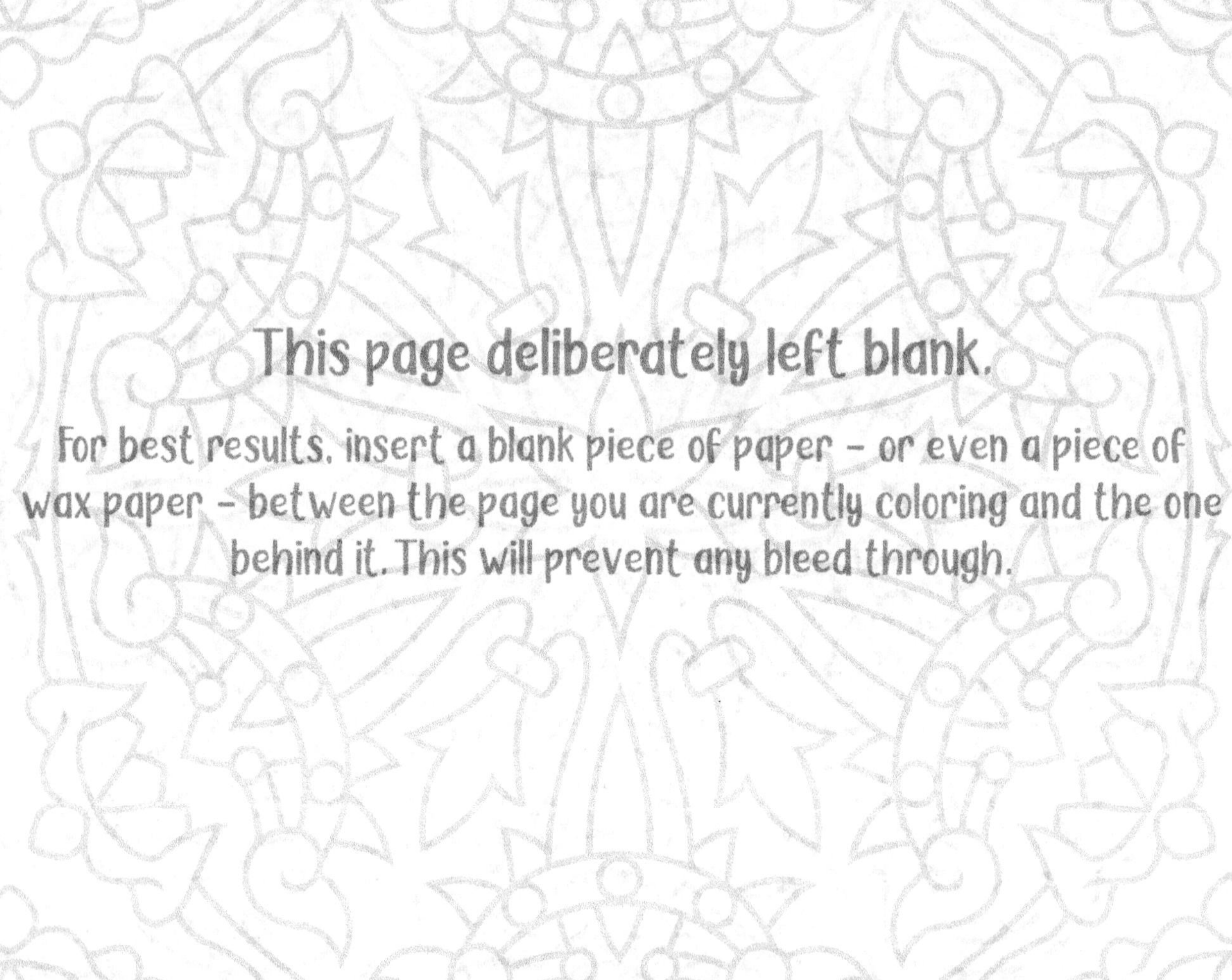

This page deliberately left blank.

For best results, insert a blank piece of paper - or even a piece of wax paper - between the page you are currently coloring and the one behind it. This will prevent any bleed through.

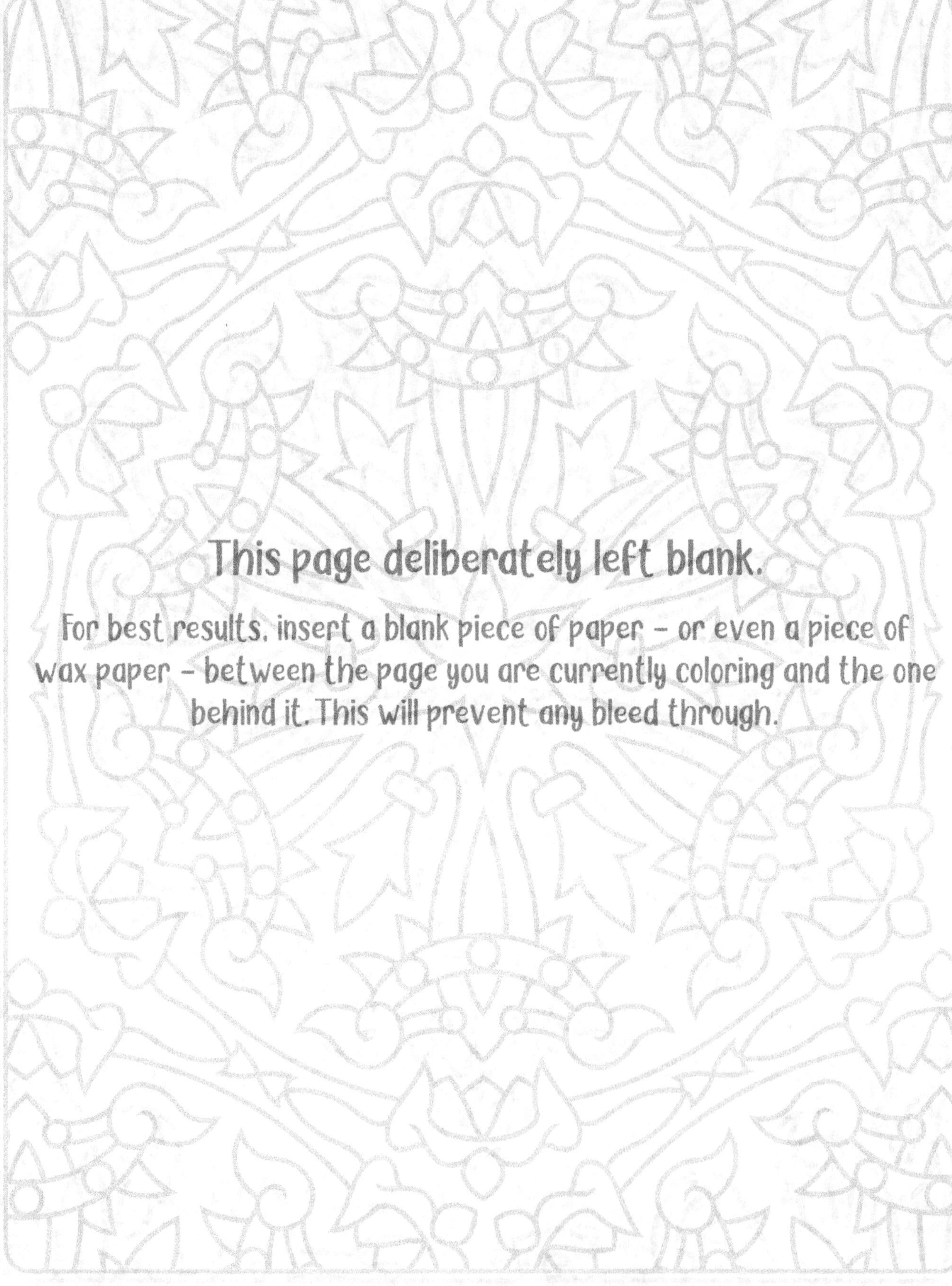

This page deliberately left blank.

For best results, insert a blank piece of paper – or even a piece of wax paper – between the page you are currently coloring and the one behind it. This will prevent any bleed through.

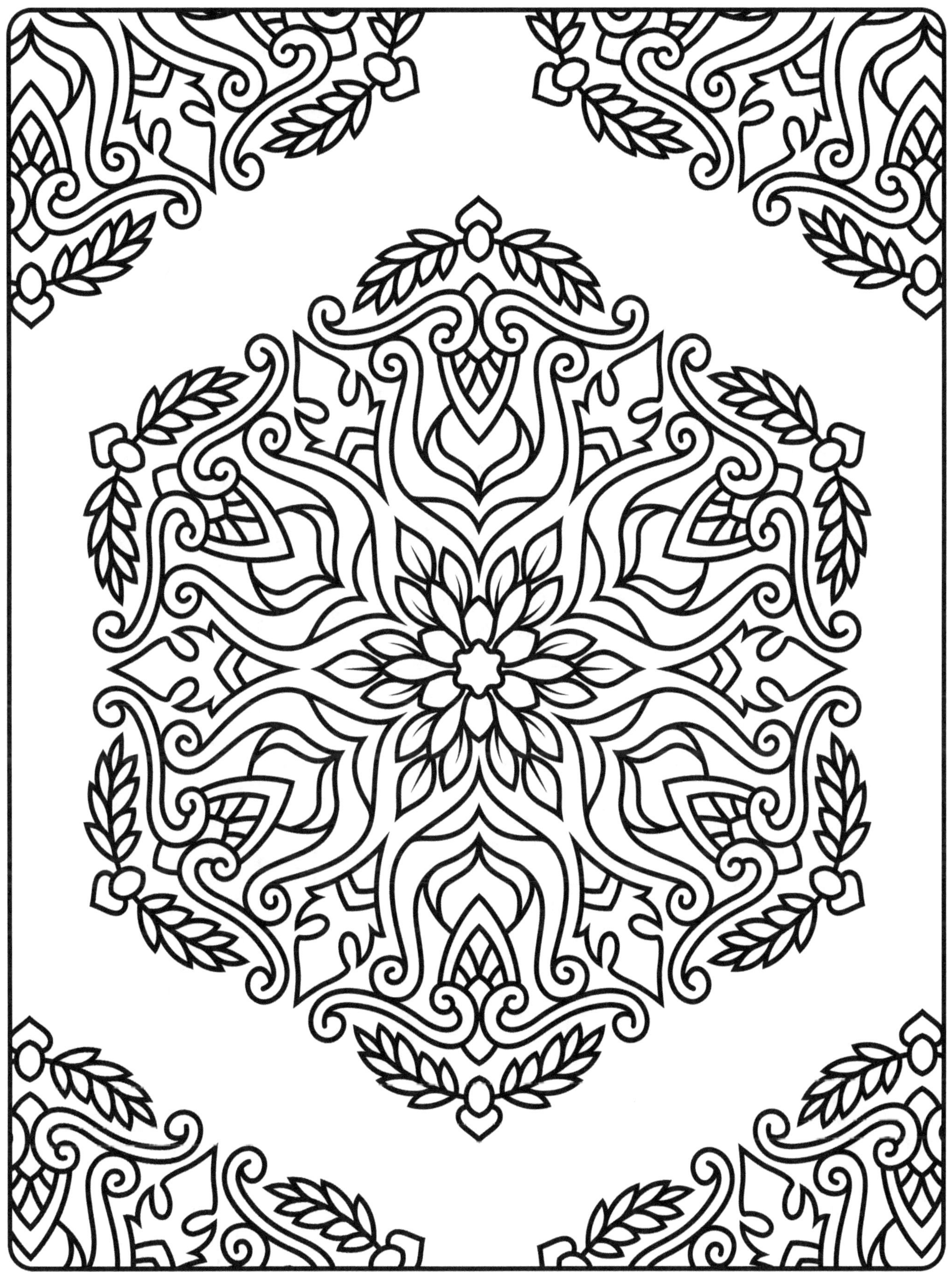

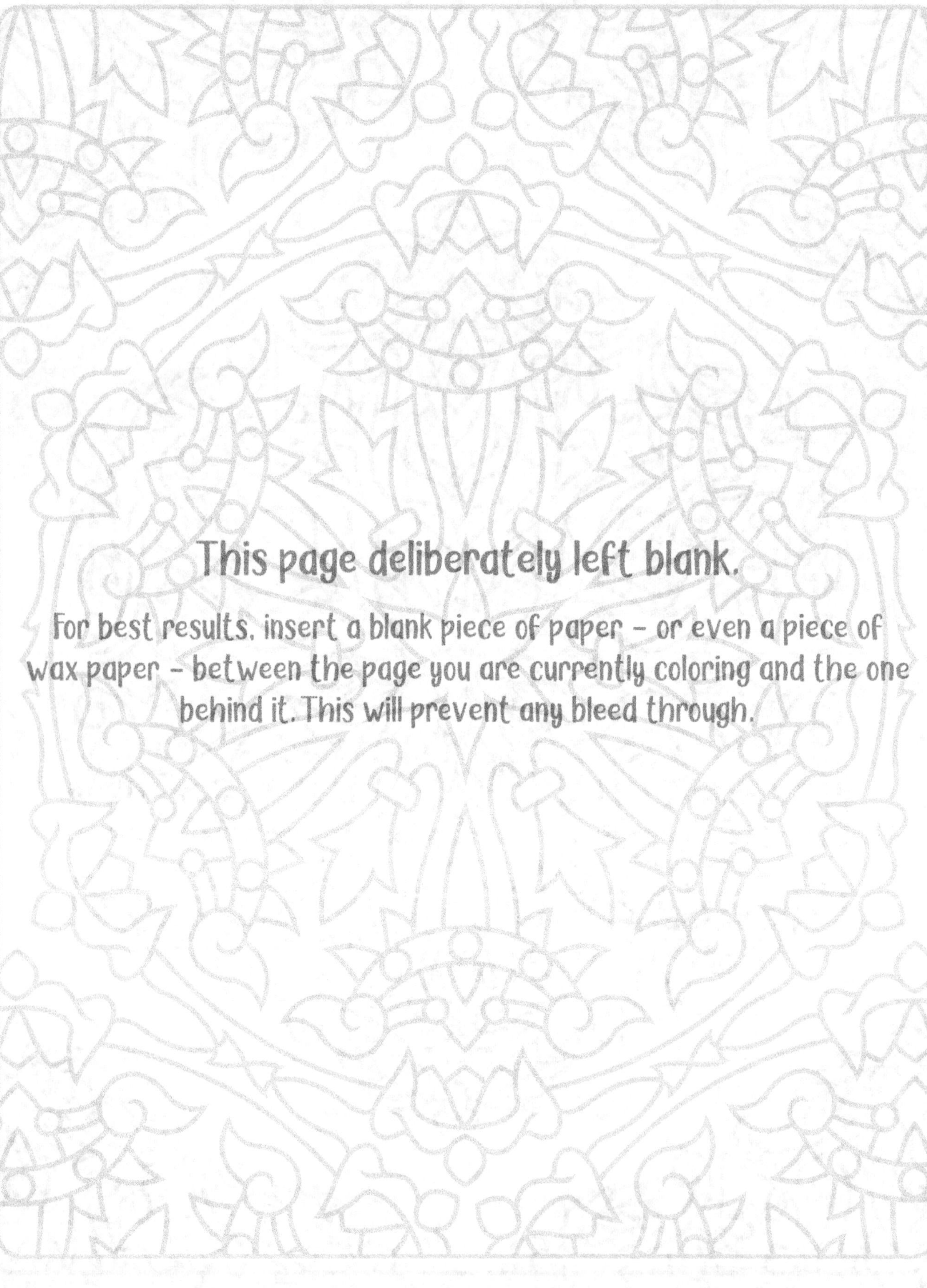

This page deliberately left blank.

For best results, insert a blank piece of paper – or even a piece of wax paper – between the page you are currently coloring and the one behind it. This will prevent any bleed through.

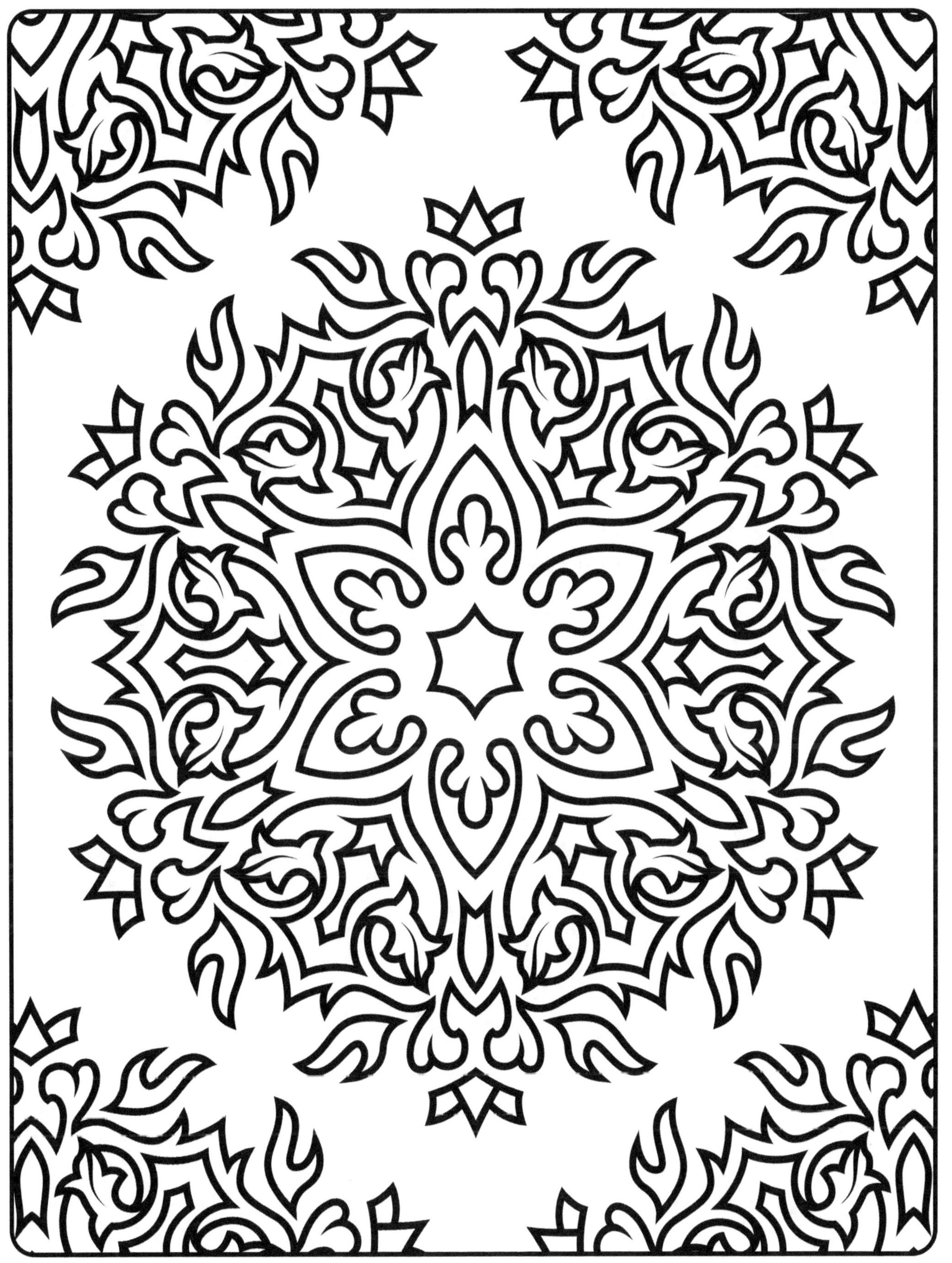

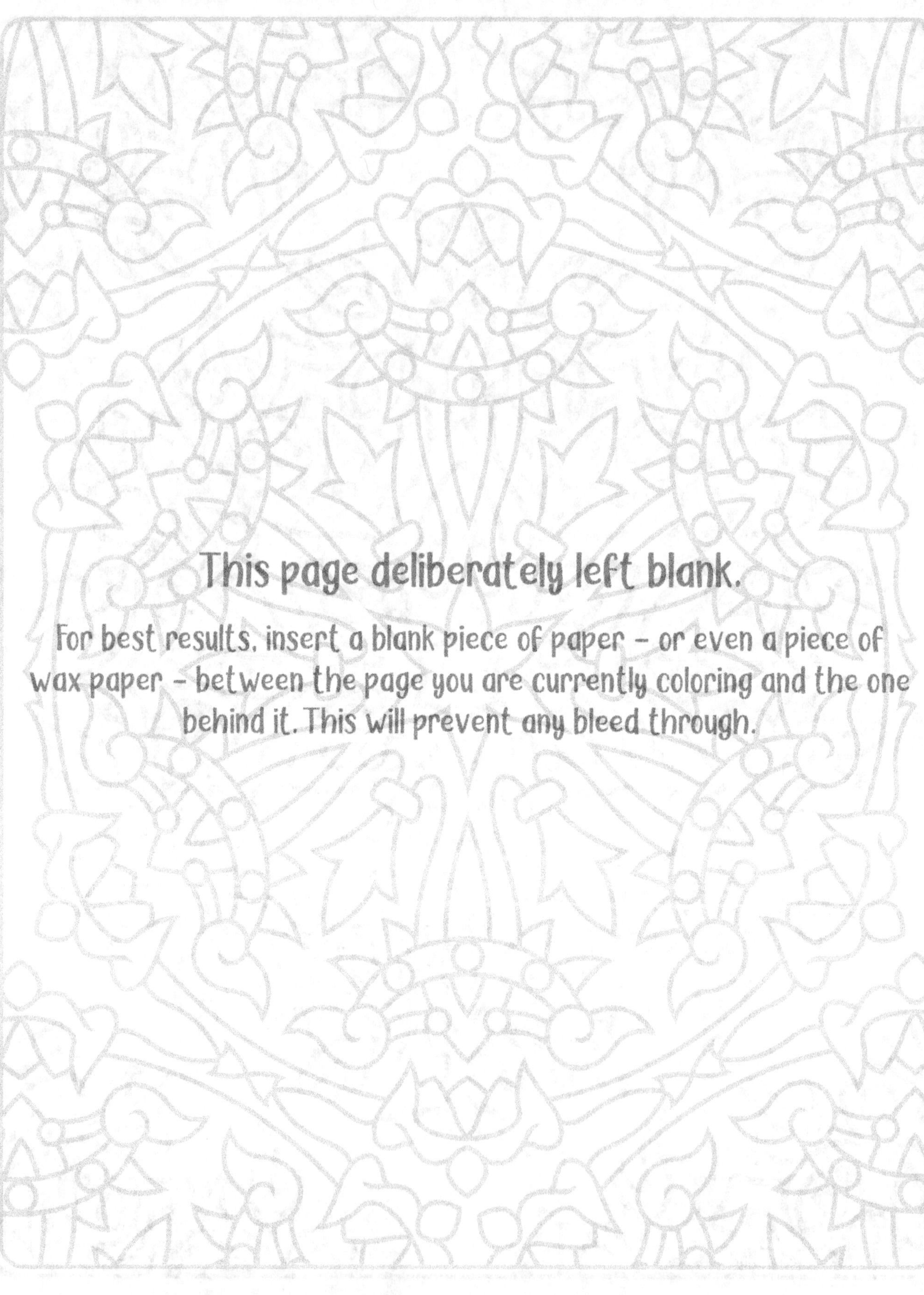

This page deliberately left blank.

For best results, insert a blank piece of paper – or even a piece of wax paper – between the page you are currently coloring and the one behind it. This will prevent any bleed through.

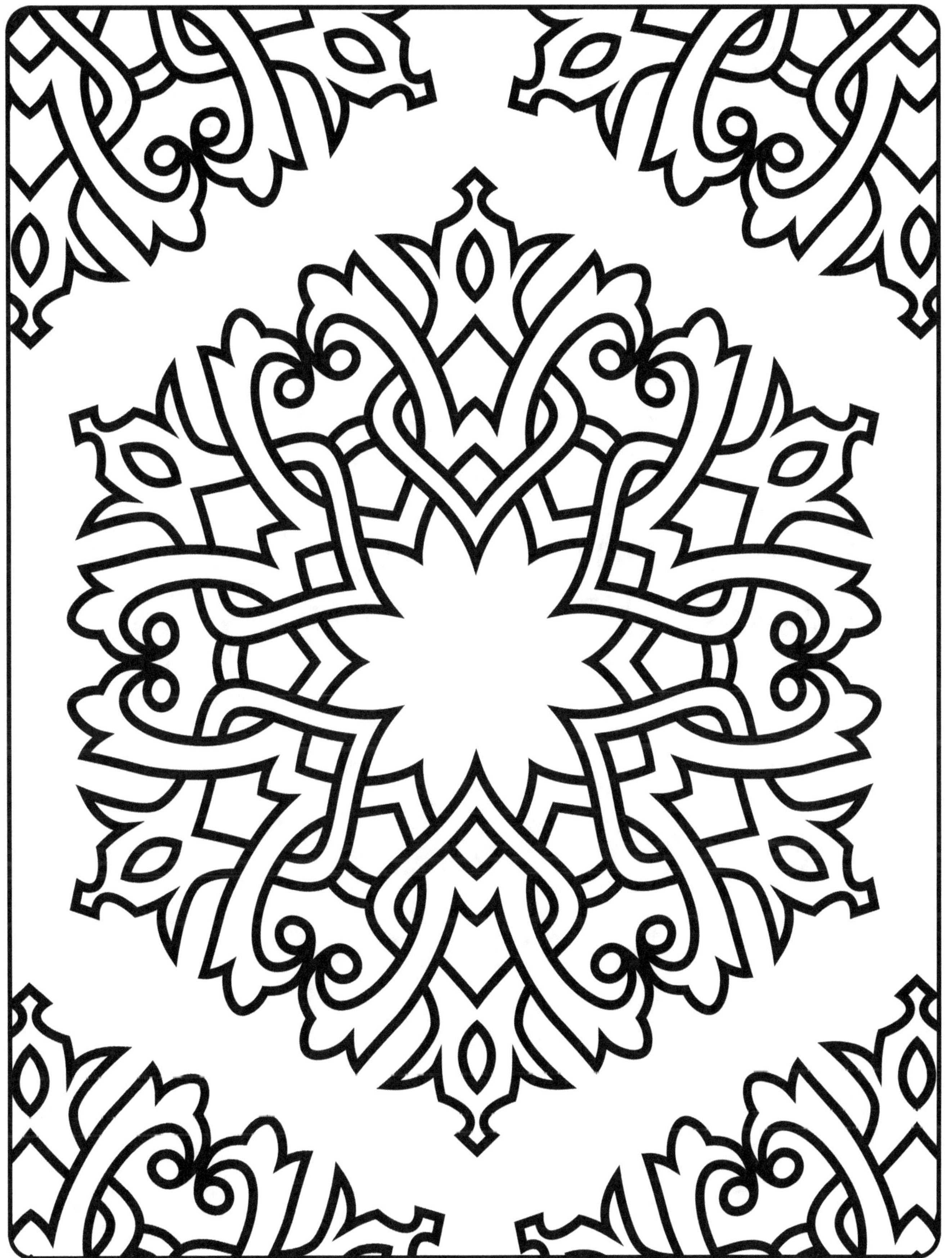

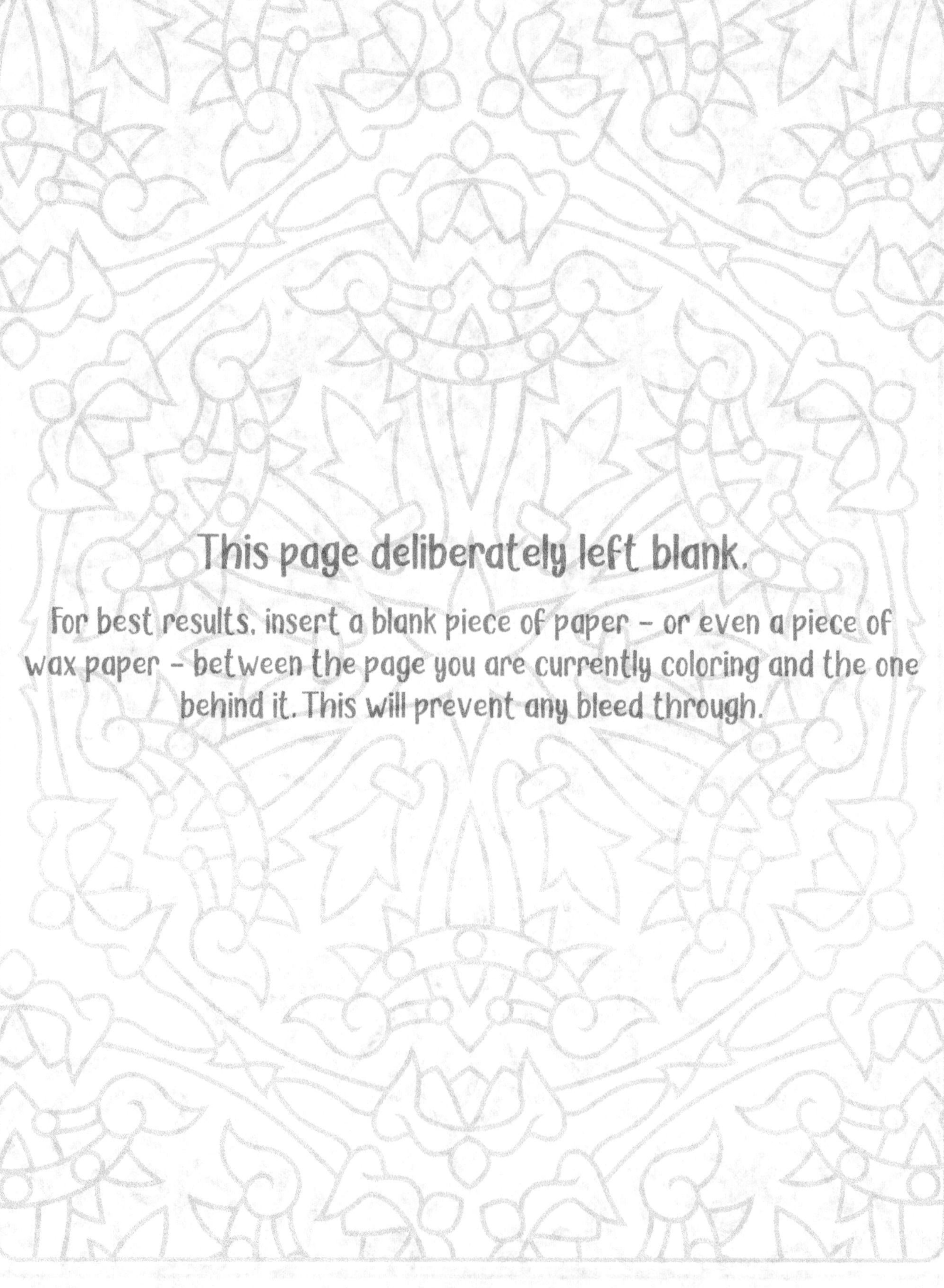

This page deliberately left blank.

For best results, insert a blank piece of paper – or even a piece of wax paper – between the page you are currently coloring and the one behind it. This will prevent any bleed through.

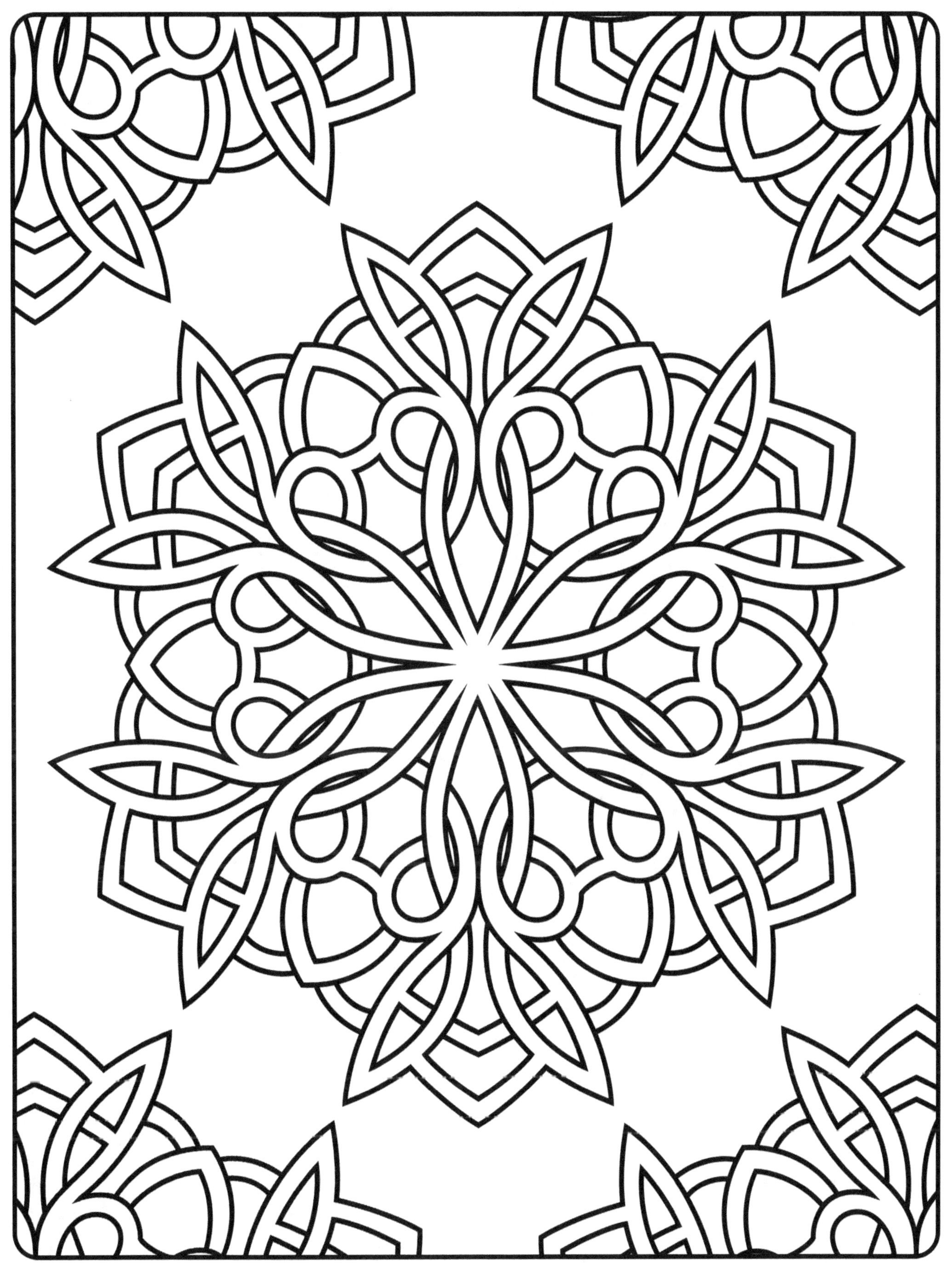

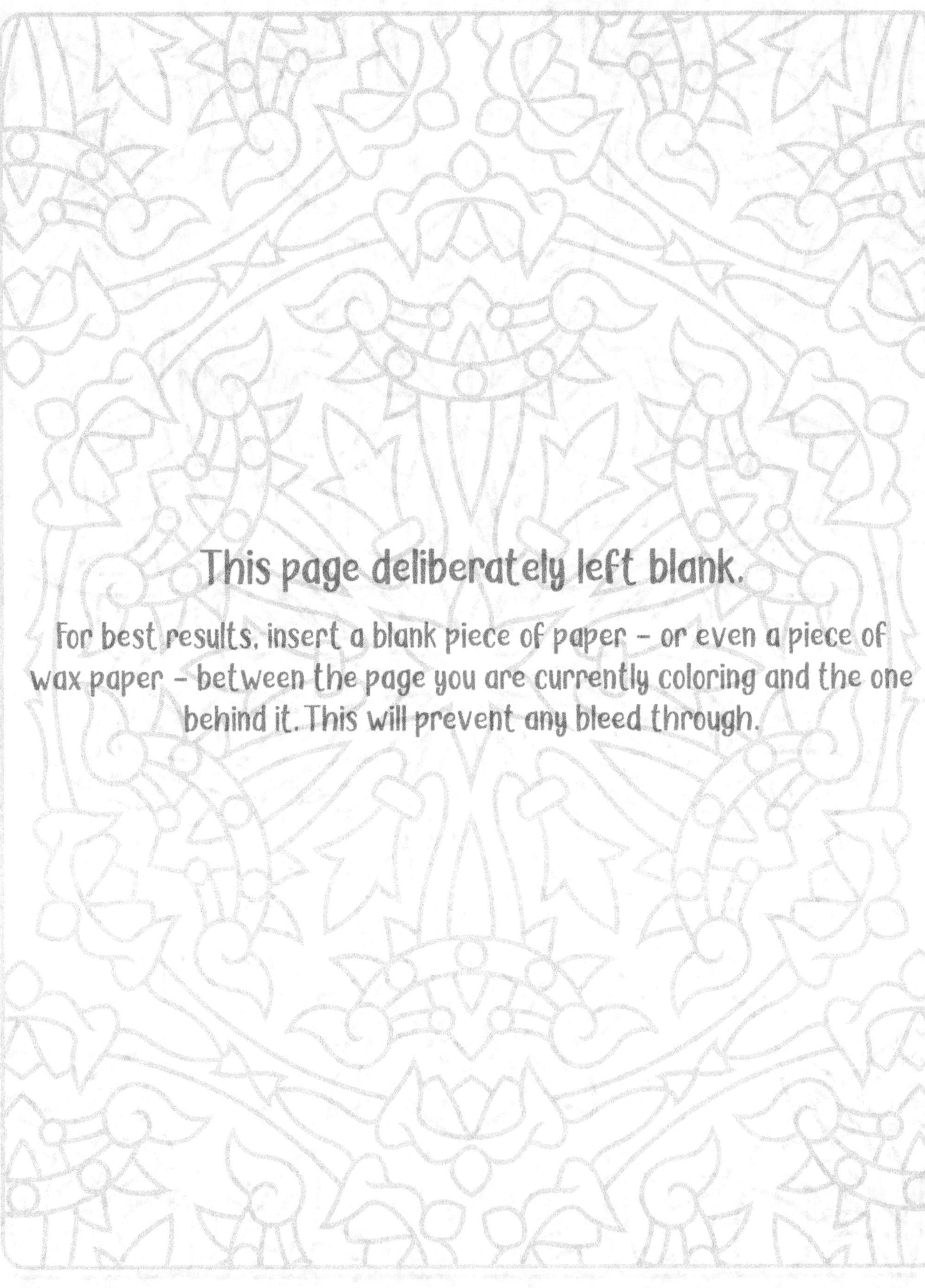

This page deliberately left blank.

For best results, insert a blank piece of paper – or even a piece of wax paper – between the page you are currently coloring and the one behind it. This will prevent any bleed through.

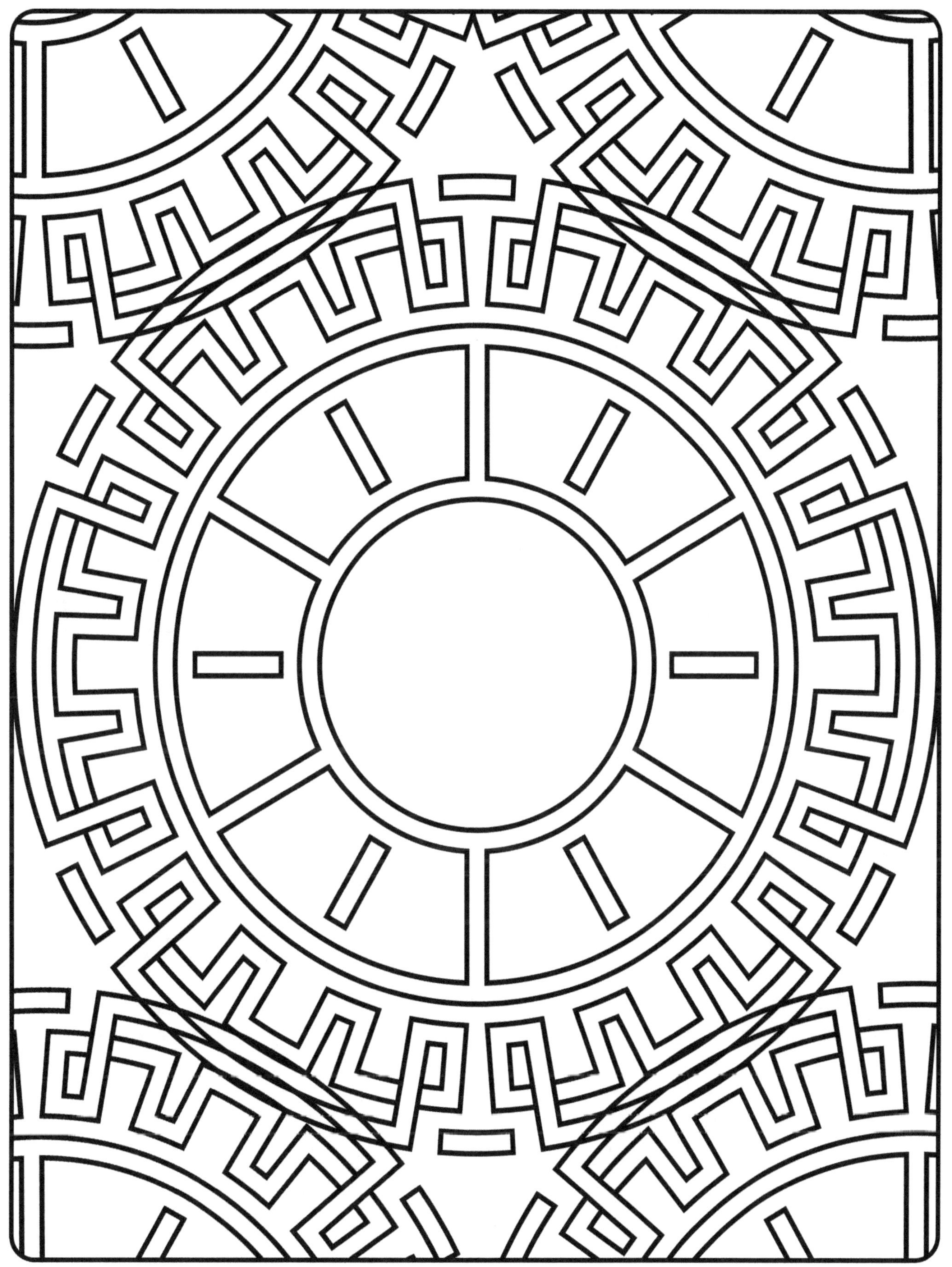

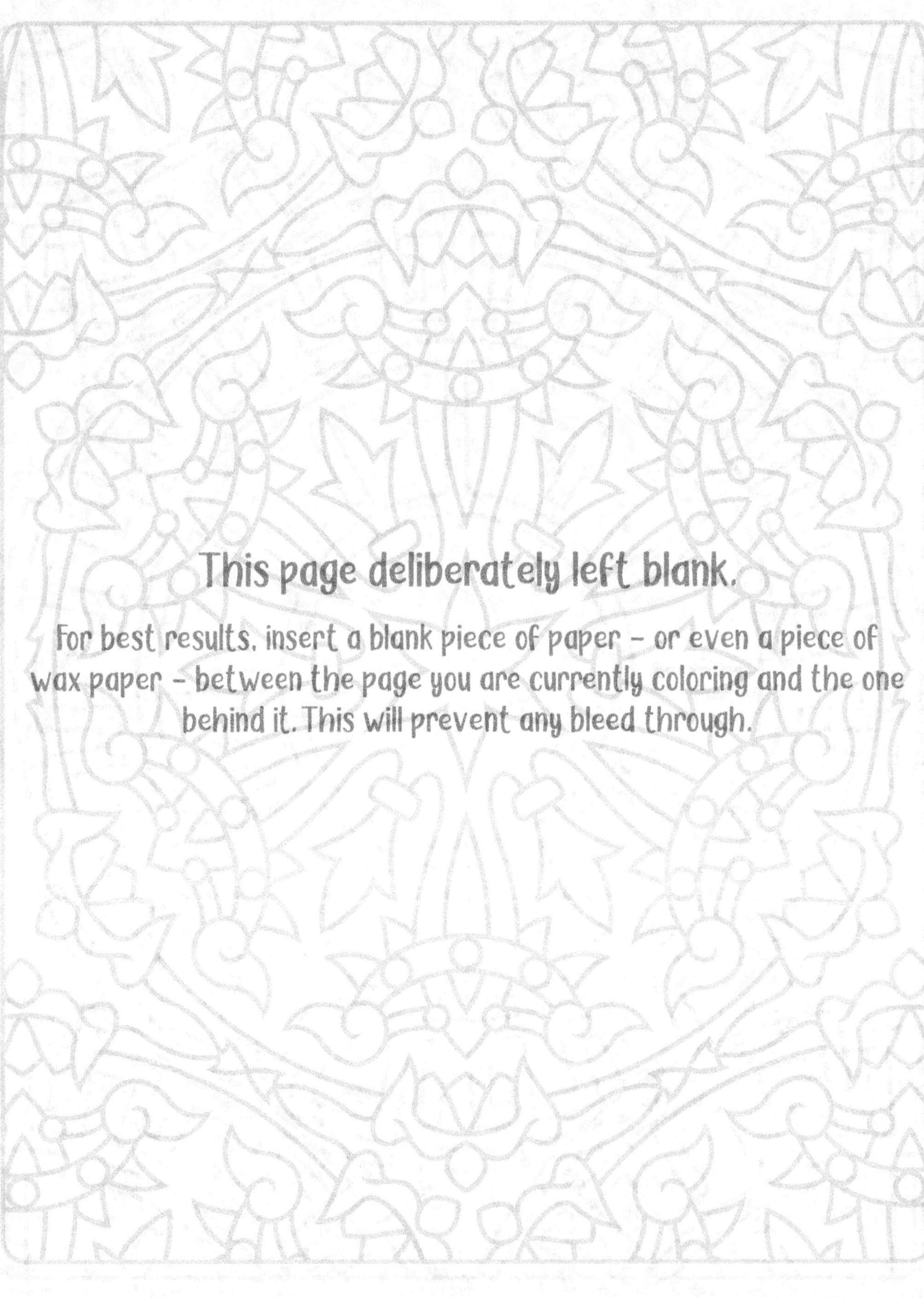

This page deliberately left blank.

For best results, insert a blank piece of paper – or even a piece of wax paper – between the page you are currently coloring and the one behind it. This will prevent any bleed through.

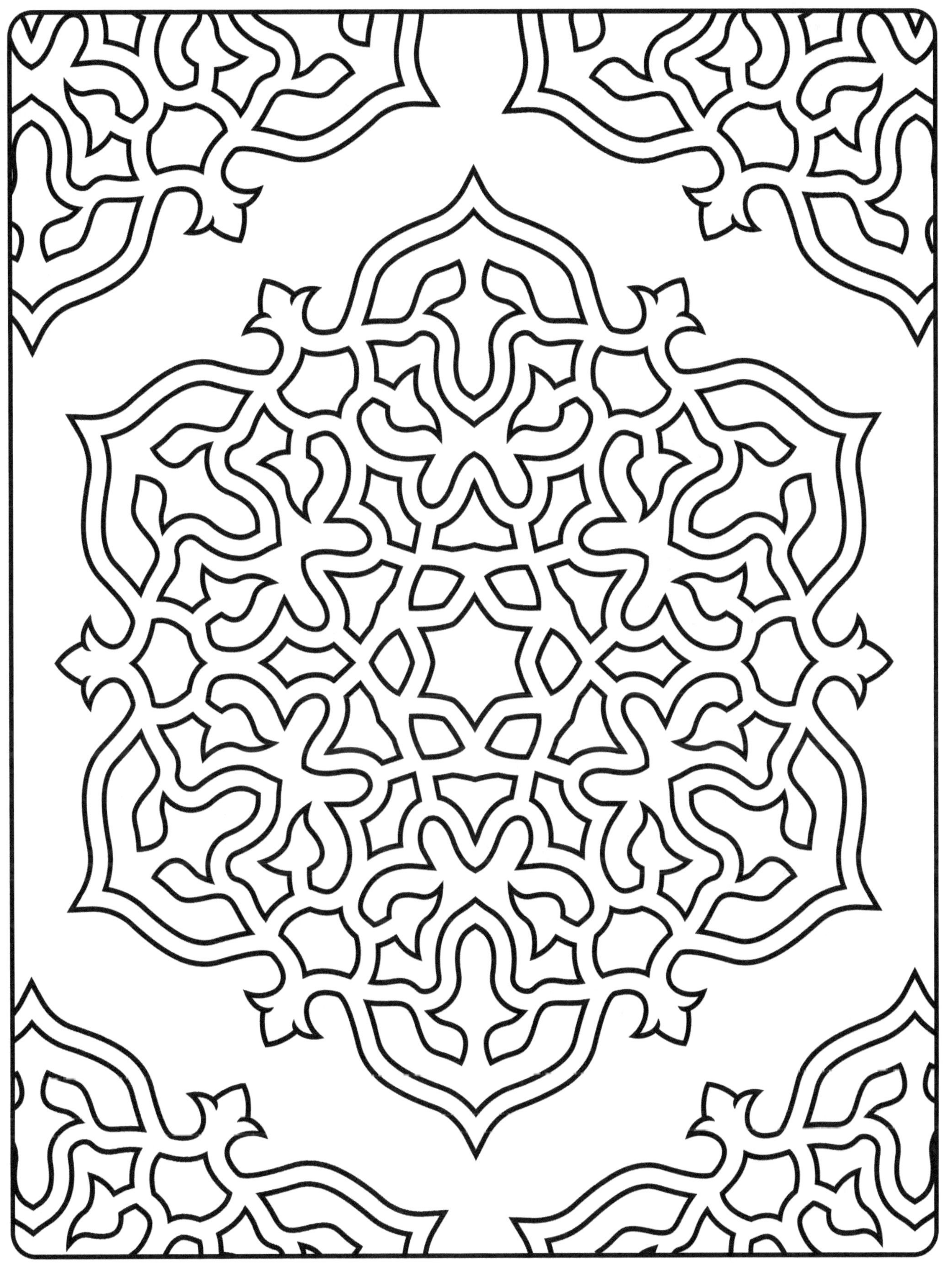

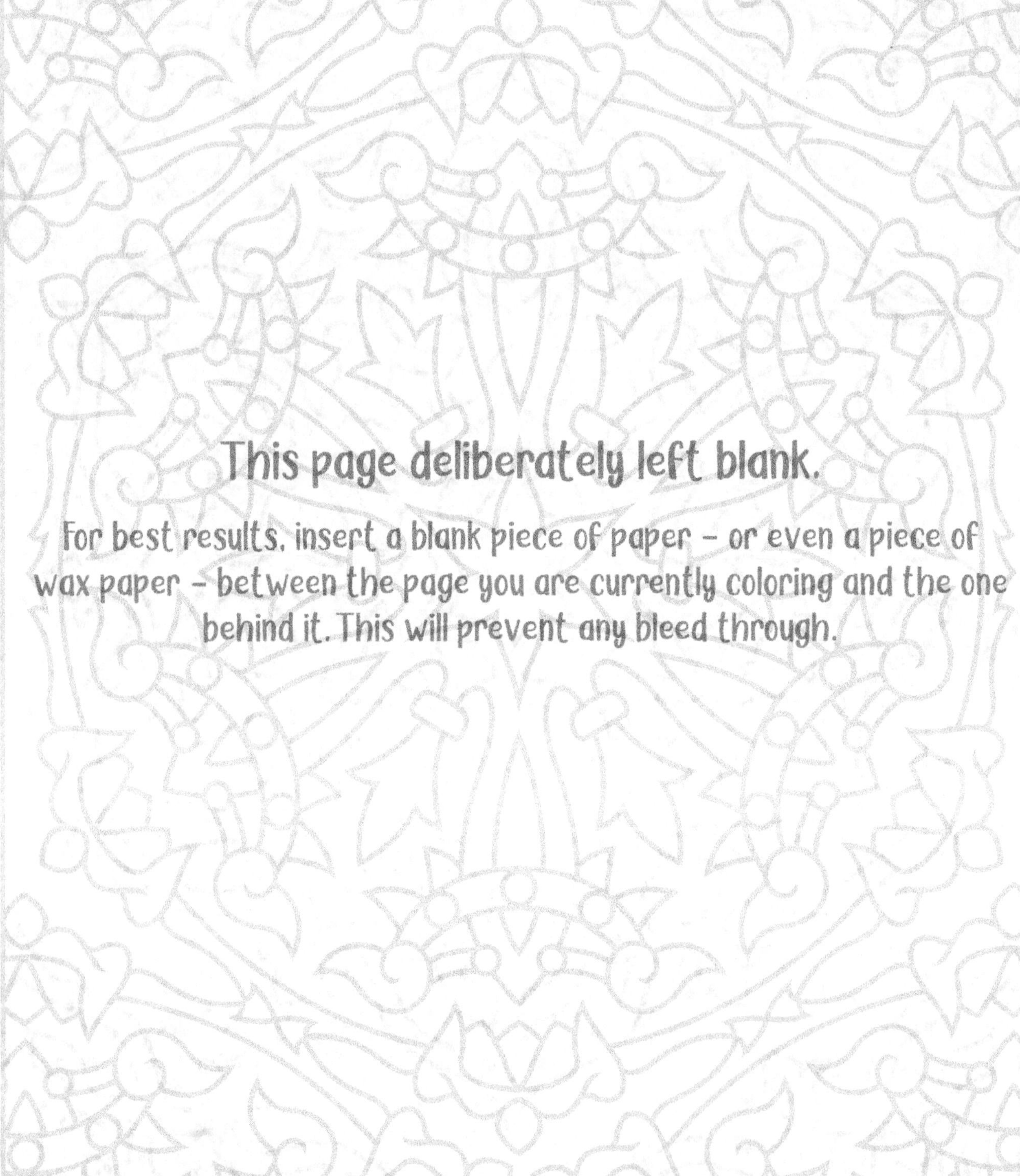

This page deliberately left blank.

For best results, insert a blank piece of paper – or even a piece of wax paper – between the page you are currently coloring and the one behind it. This will prevent any bleed through.

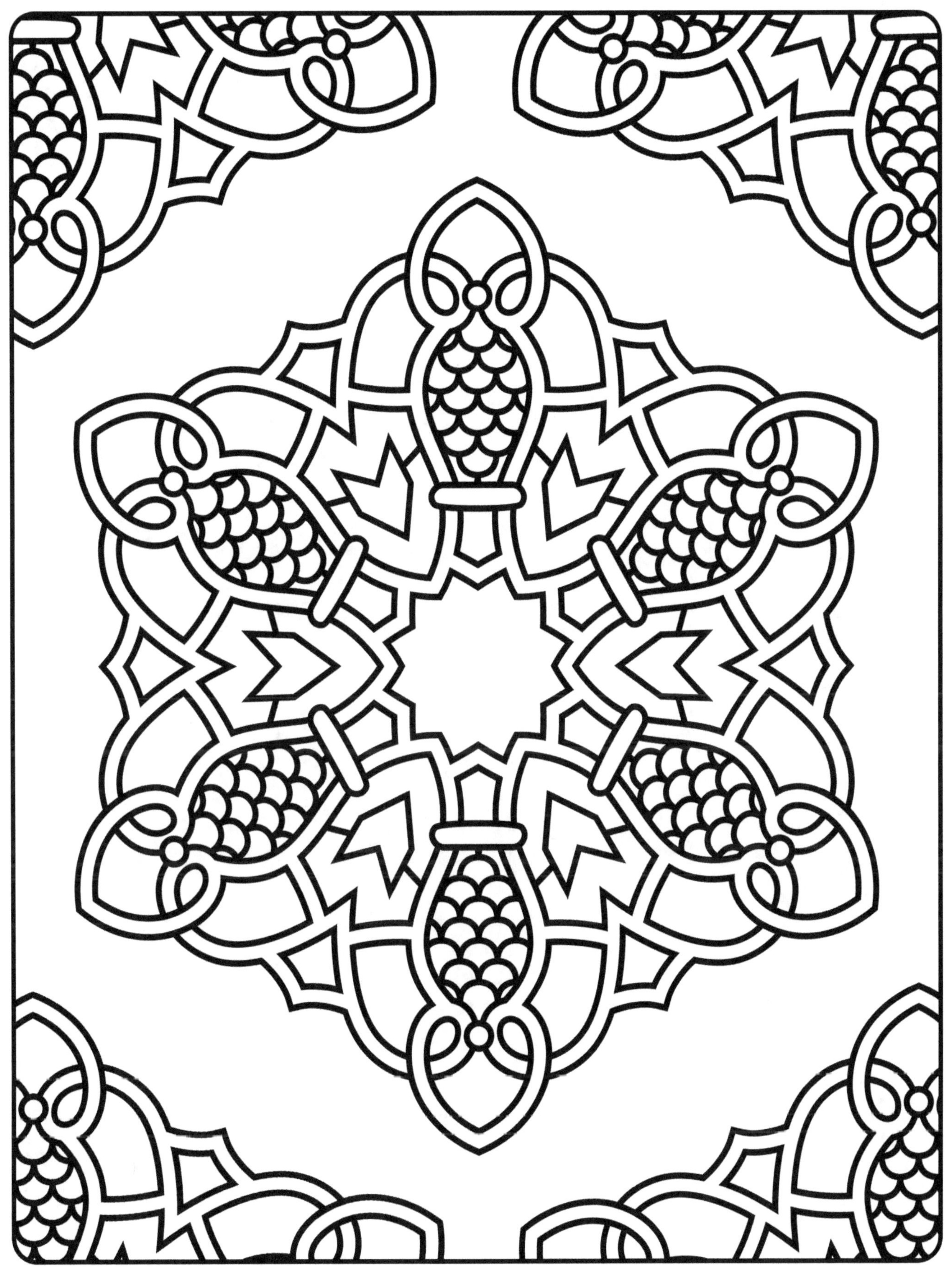

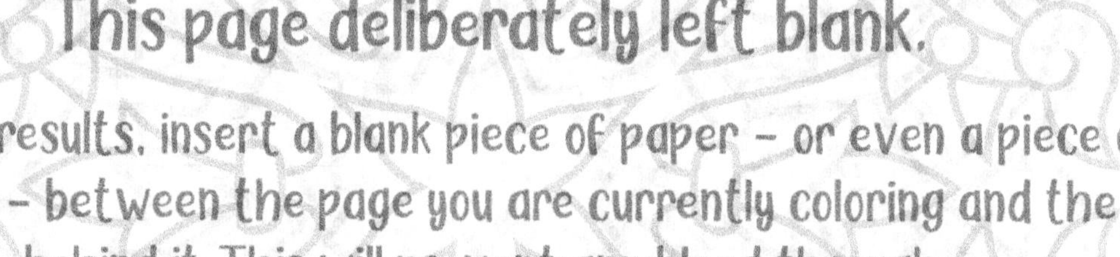

This page deliberately left blank.

For best results, insert a blank piece of paper – or even a piece of wax paper – between the page you are currently coloring and the one behind it. This will prevent any bleed through.

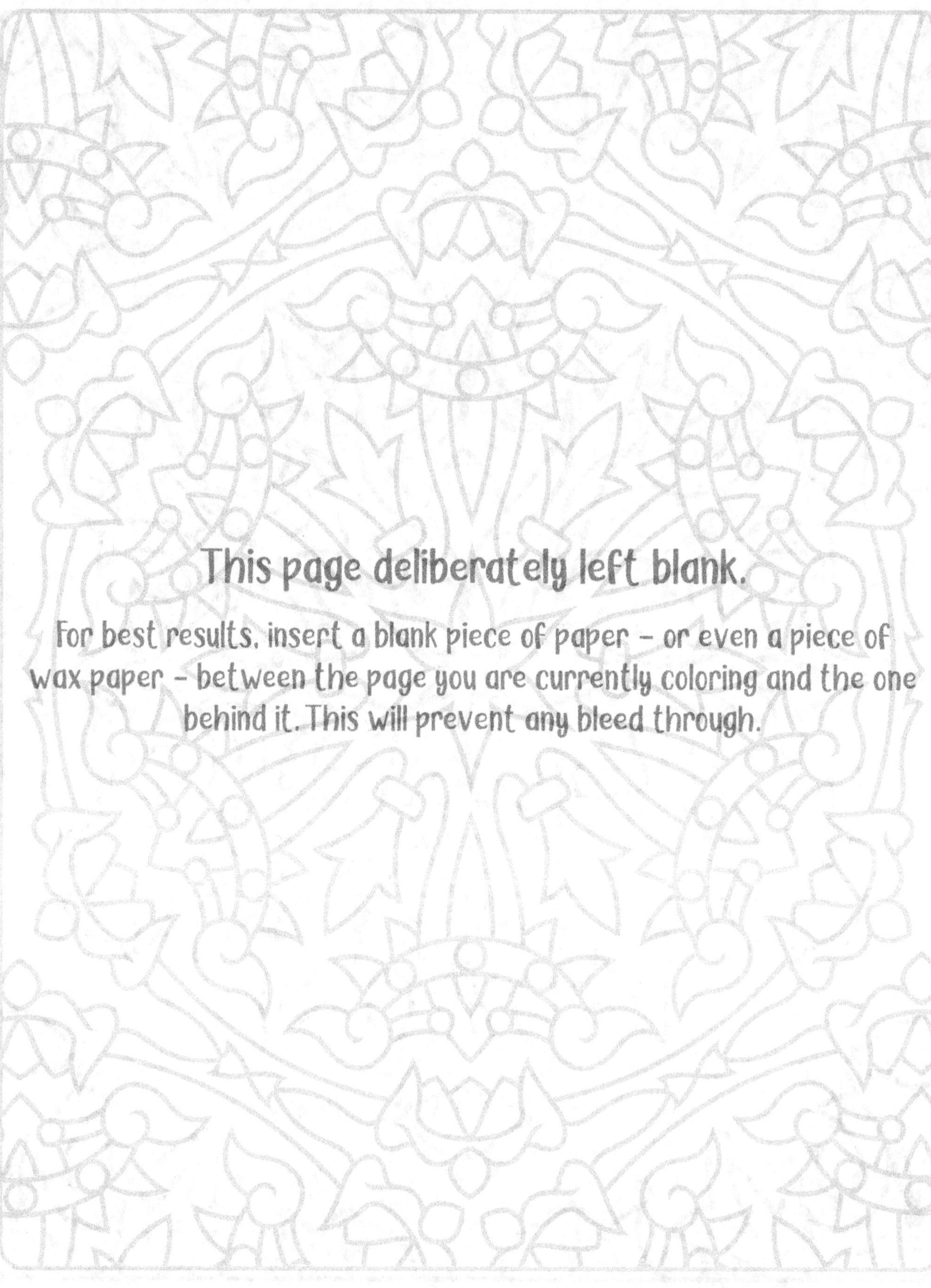

This page deliberately left blank.

For best results, insert a blank piece of paper – or even a piece of wax paper – between the page you are currently coloring and the one behind it. This will prevent any bleed through.

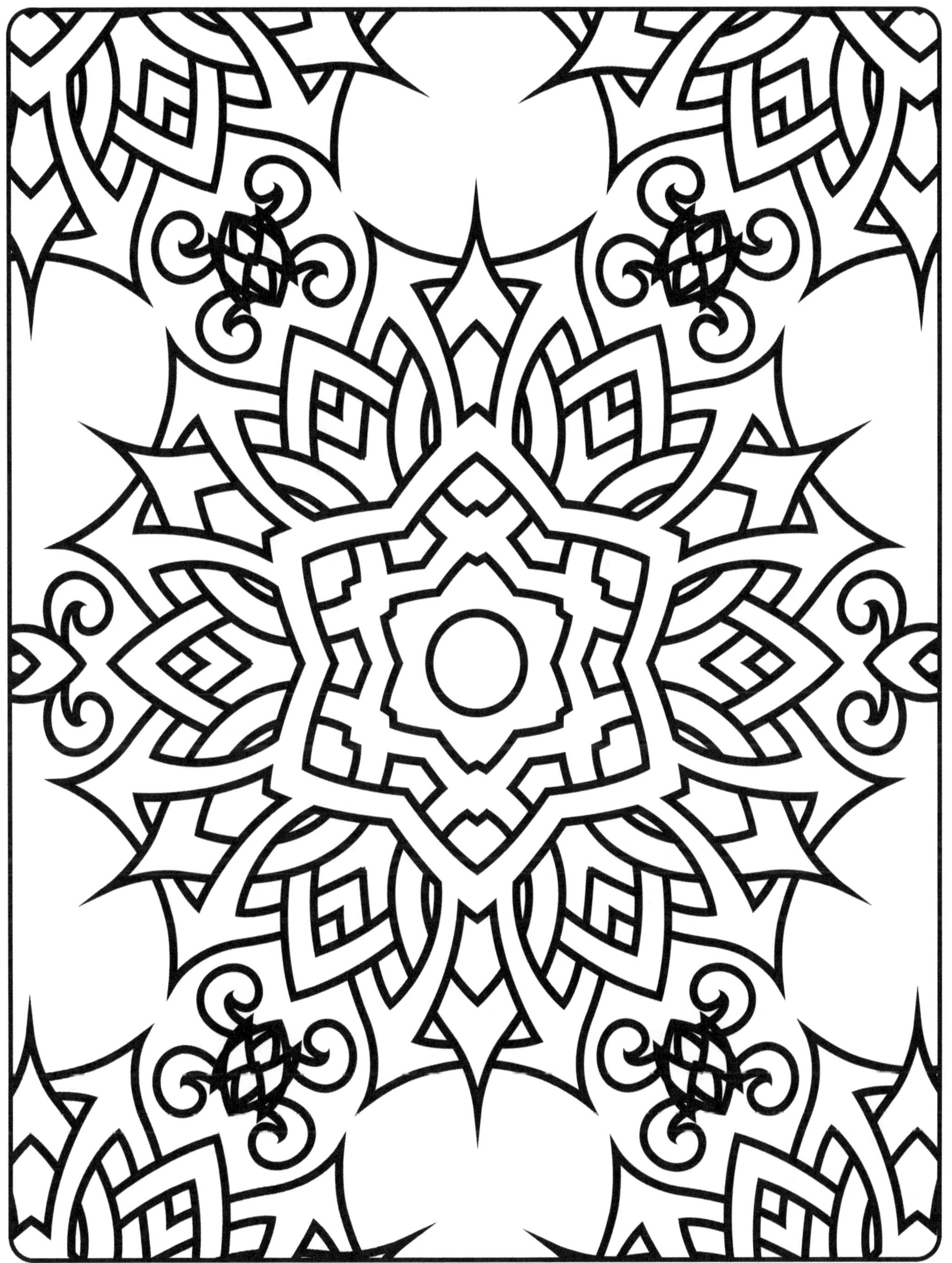

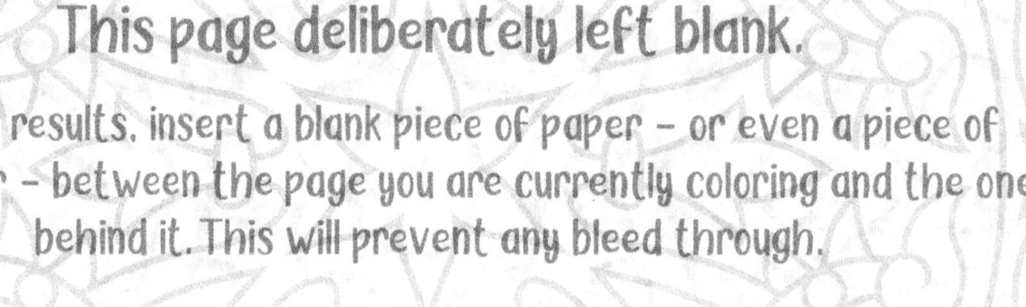

This page deliberately left blank.

For best results, insert a blank piece of paper – or even a piece of wax paper – between the page you are currently coloring and the one behind it. This will prevent any bleed through.

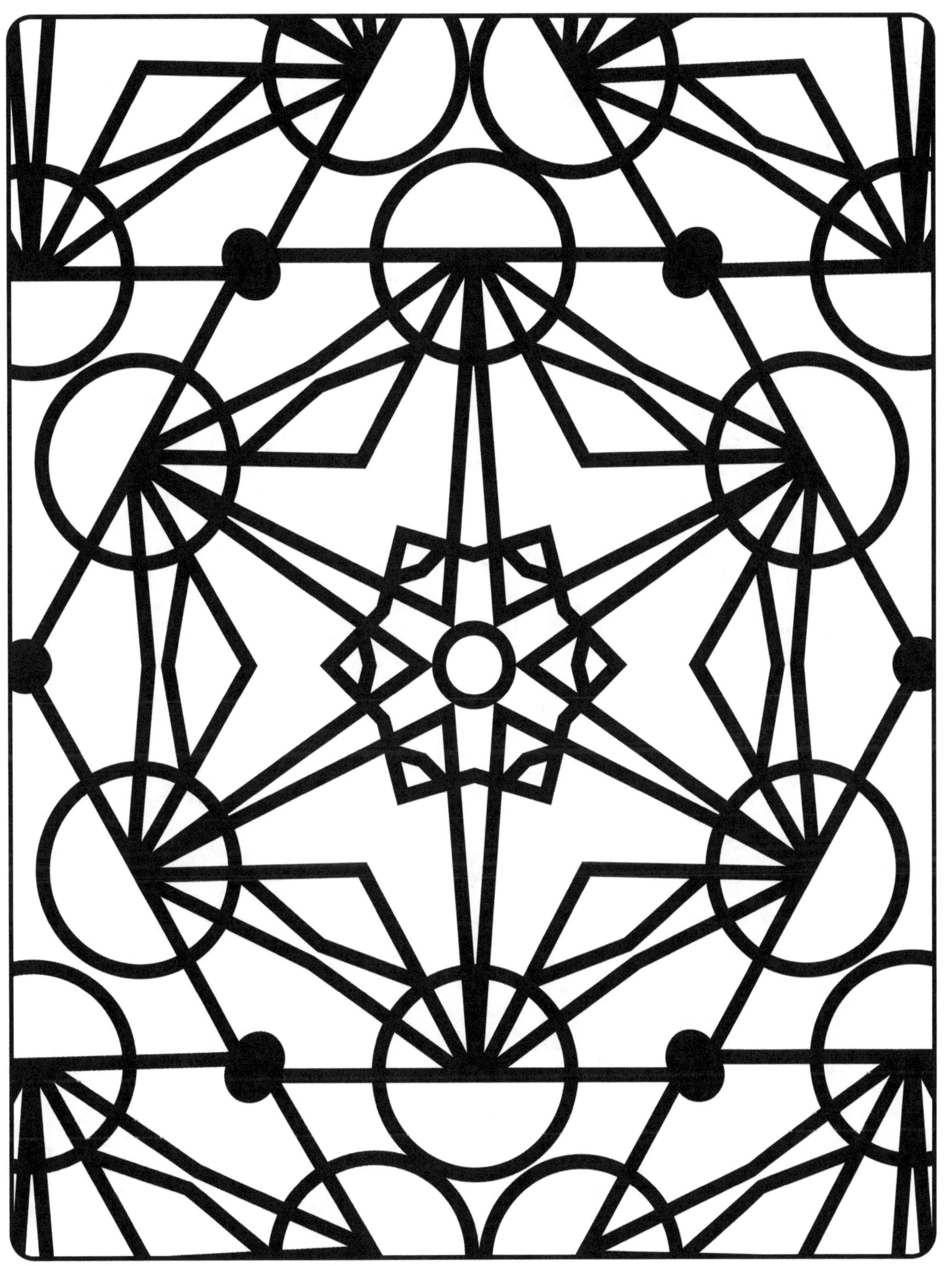

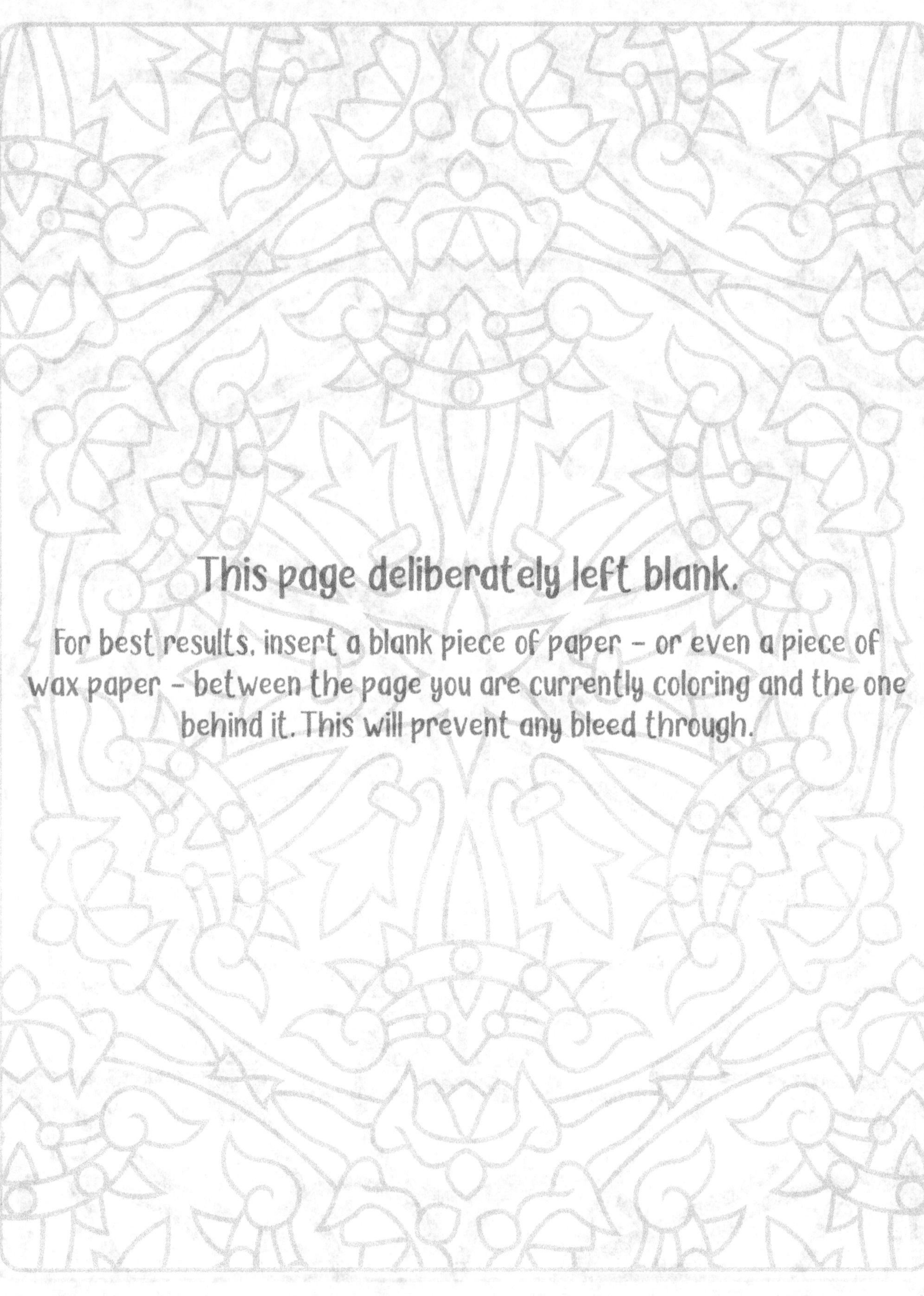

This page deliberately left blank.

For best results, insert a blank piece of paper – or even a piece of wax paper – between the page you are currently coloring and the one behind it. This will prevent any bleed through.

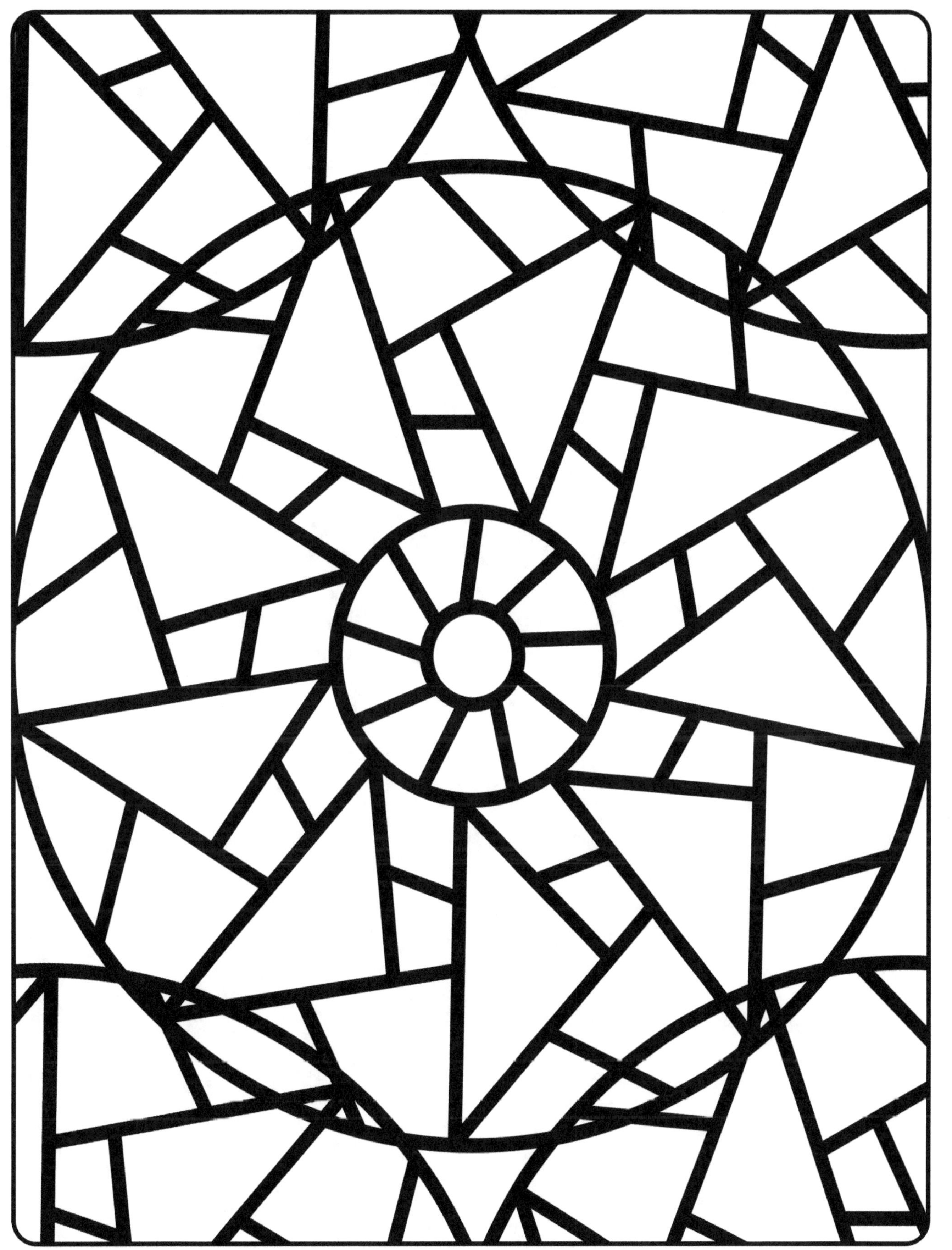

This page deliberately left blank.

For best results, insert a blank piece of paper – or even a piece of wax paper – between the page you are currently coloring and the one behind it. This will prevent any bleed through.

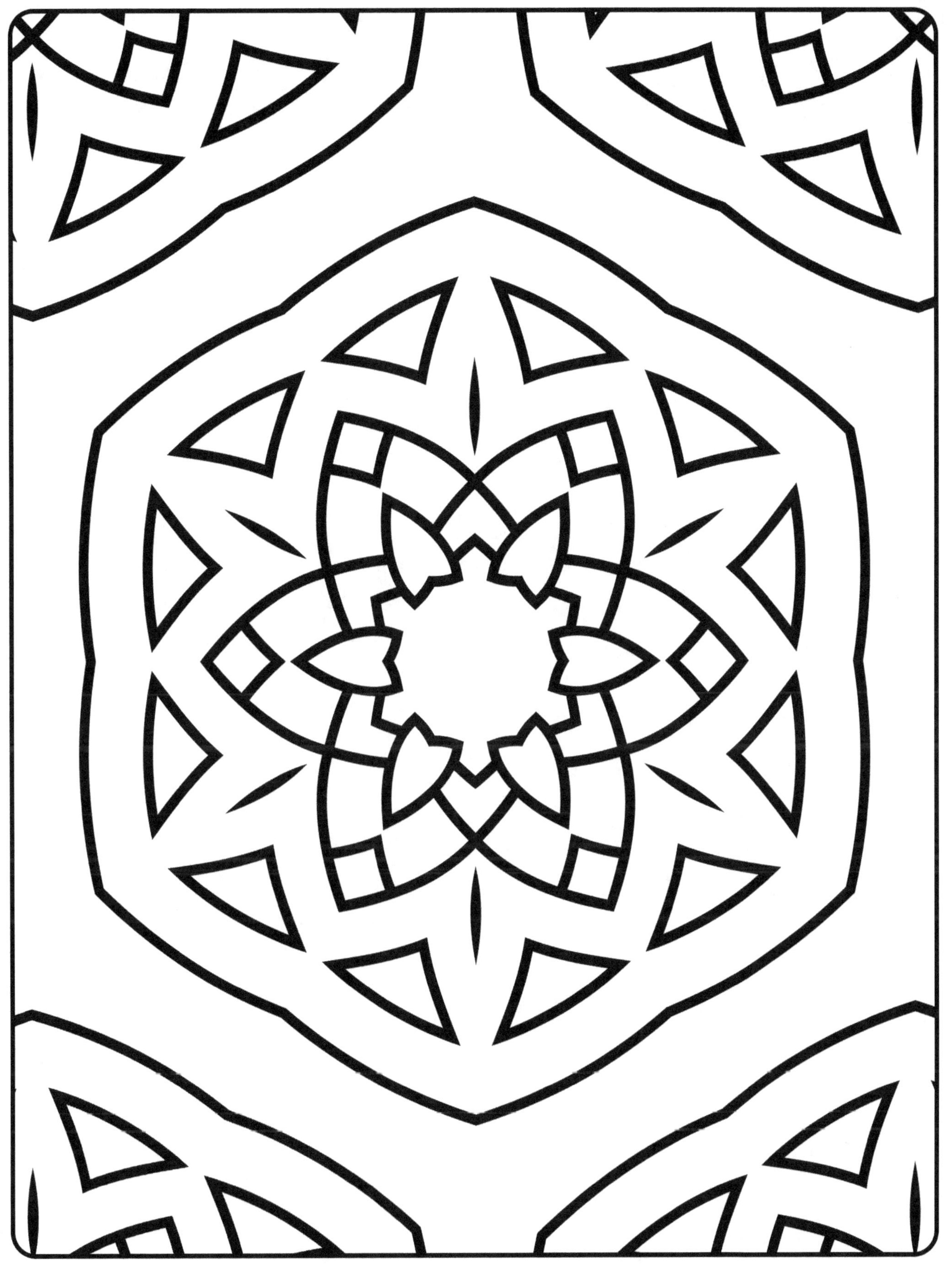

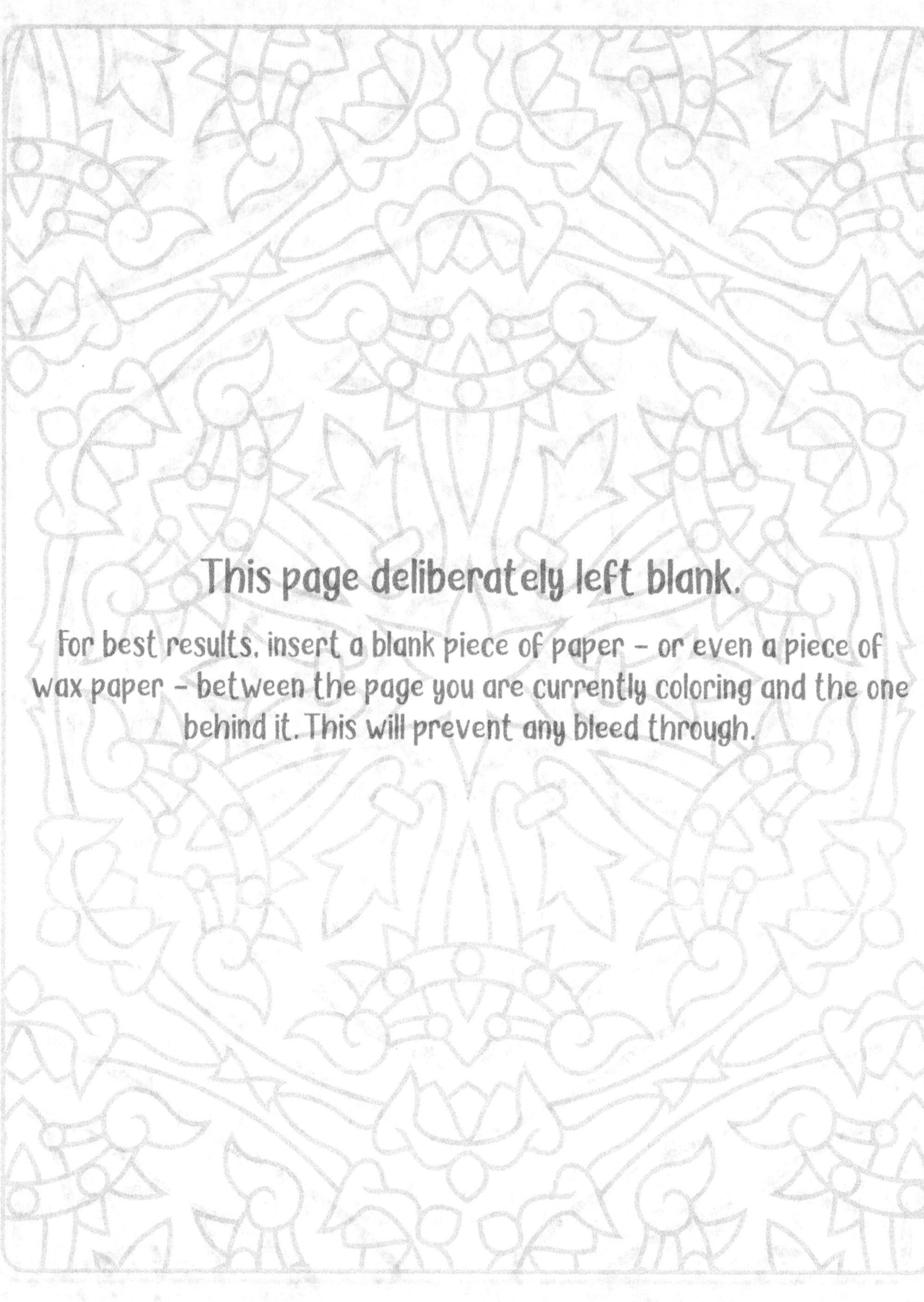

This page deliberately left blank.

For best results, insert a blank piece of paper – or even a piece of wax paper – between the page you are currently coloring and the one behind it. This will prevent any bleed through.

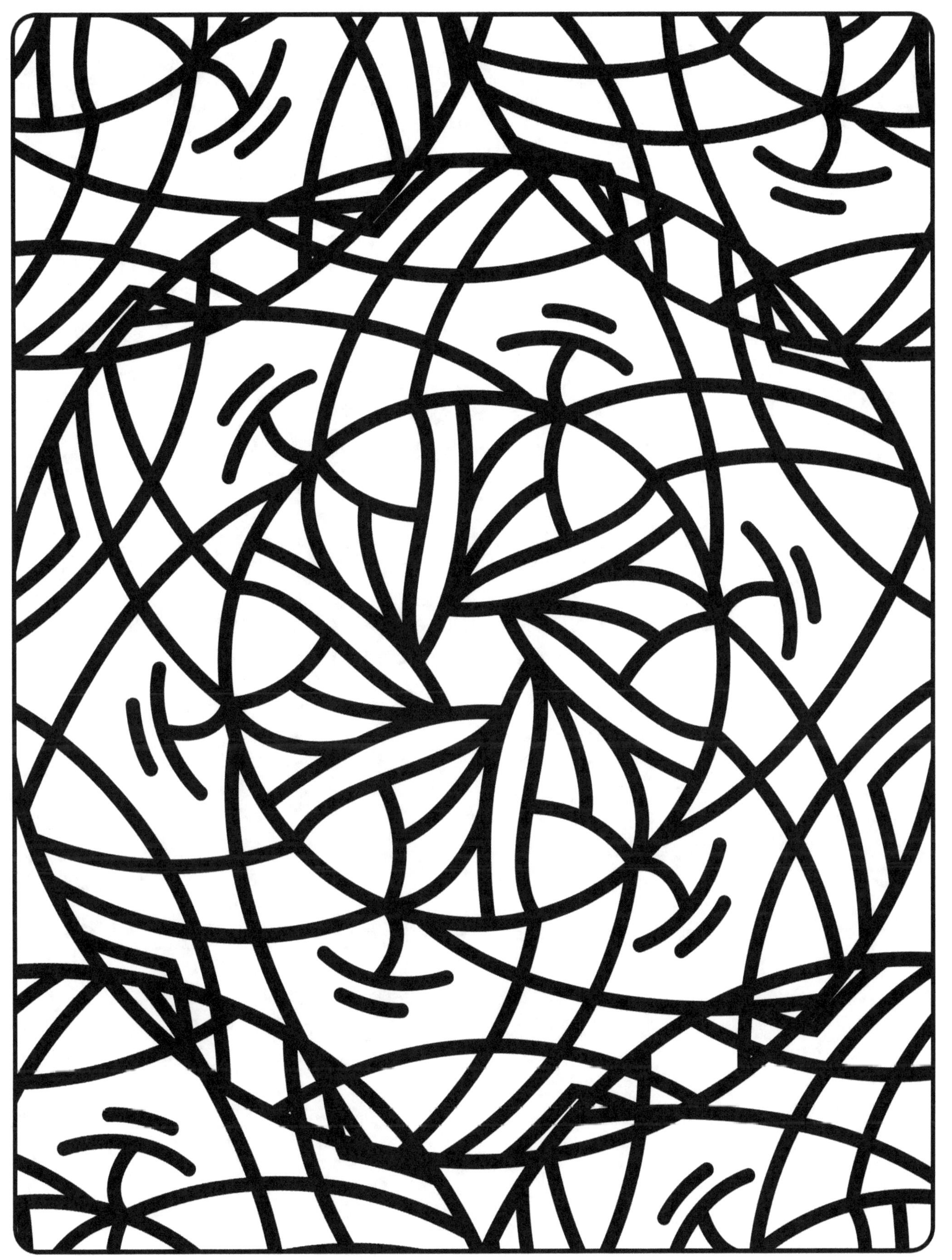

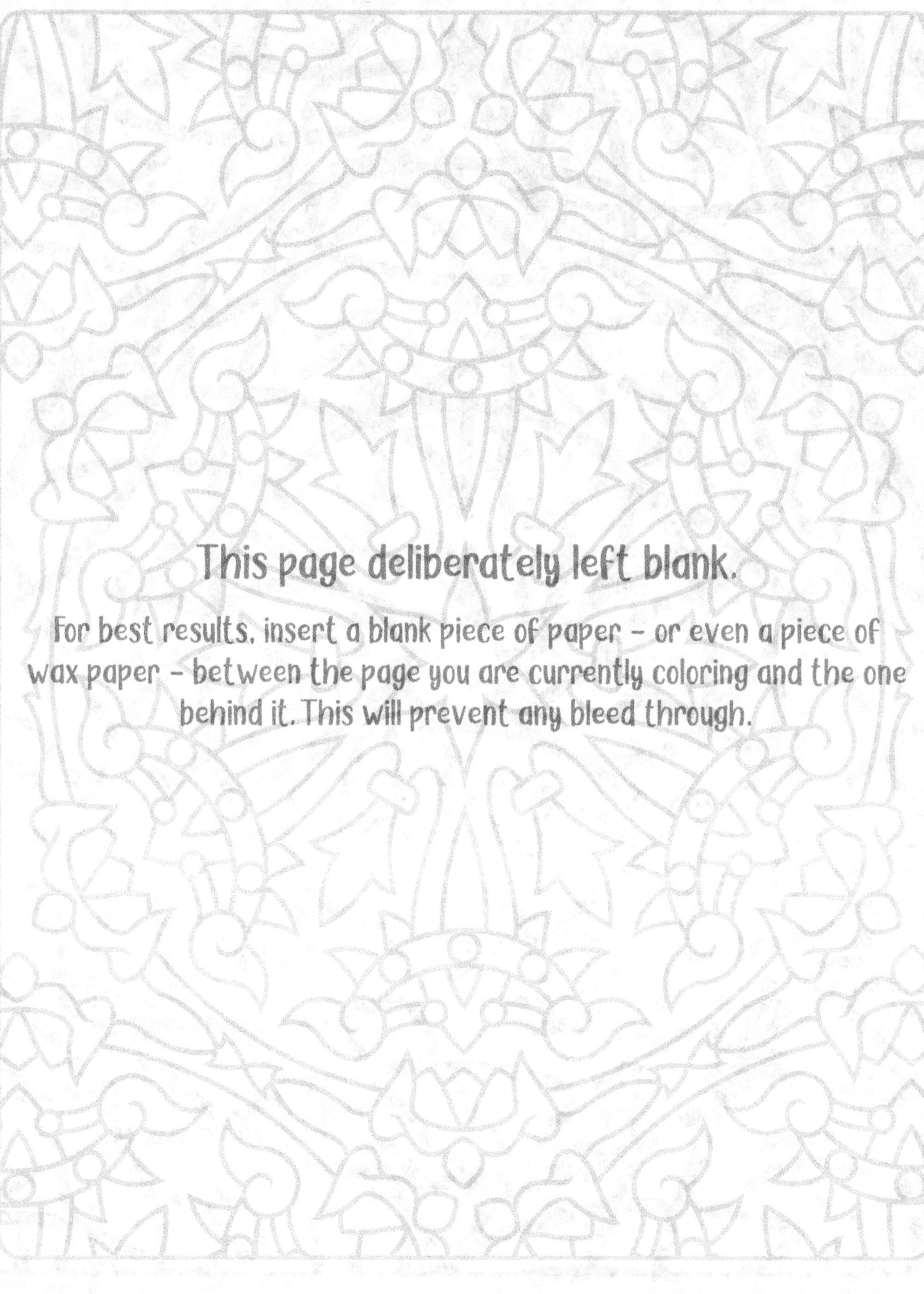

This page deliberately left blank.

For best results, insert a blank piece of paper – or even a piece of wax paper – between the page you are currently coloring and the one behind it. This will prevent any bleed through.

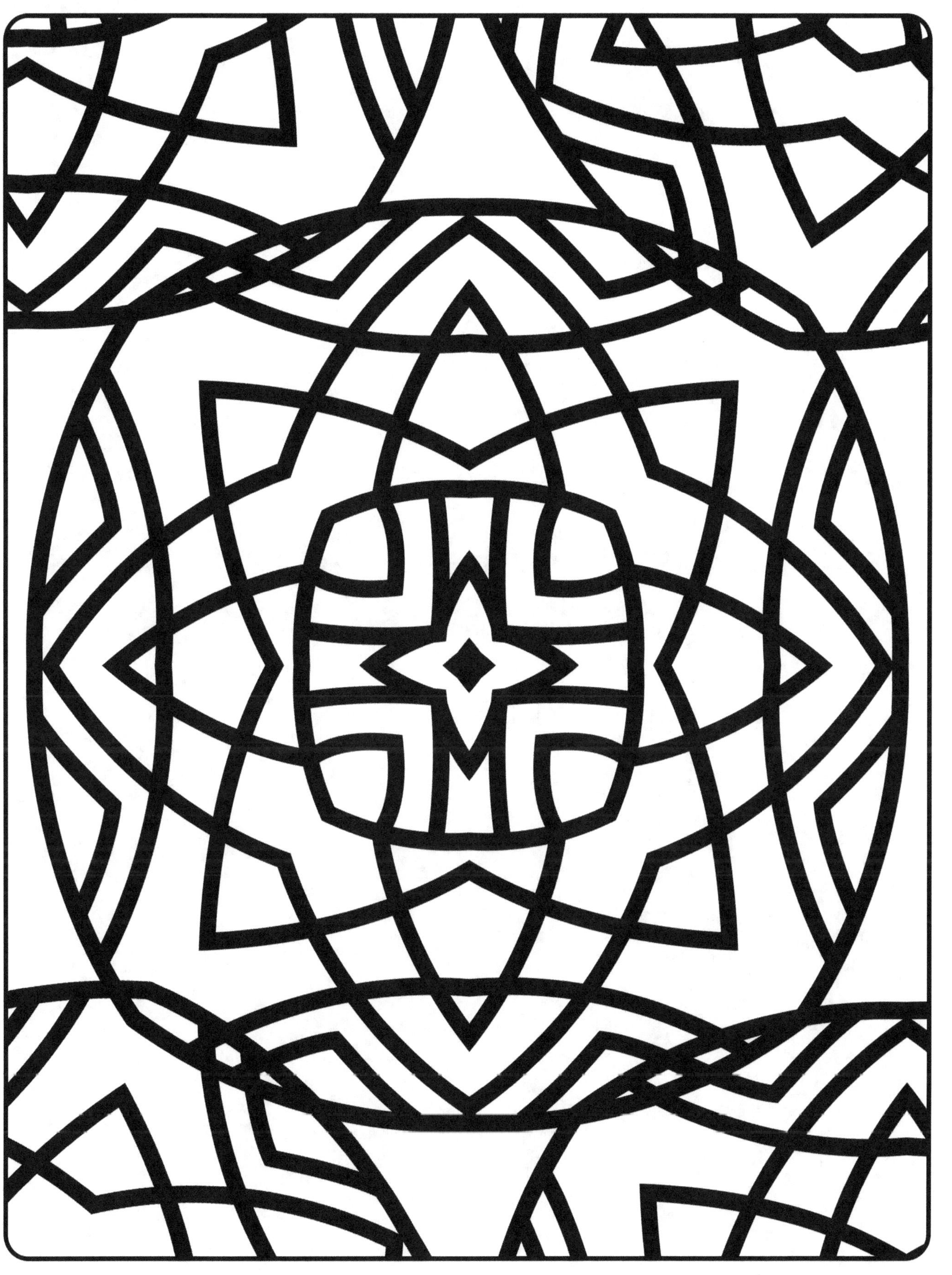

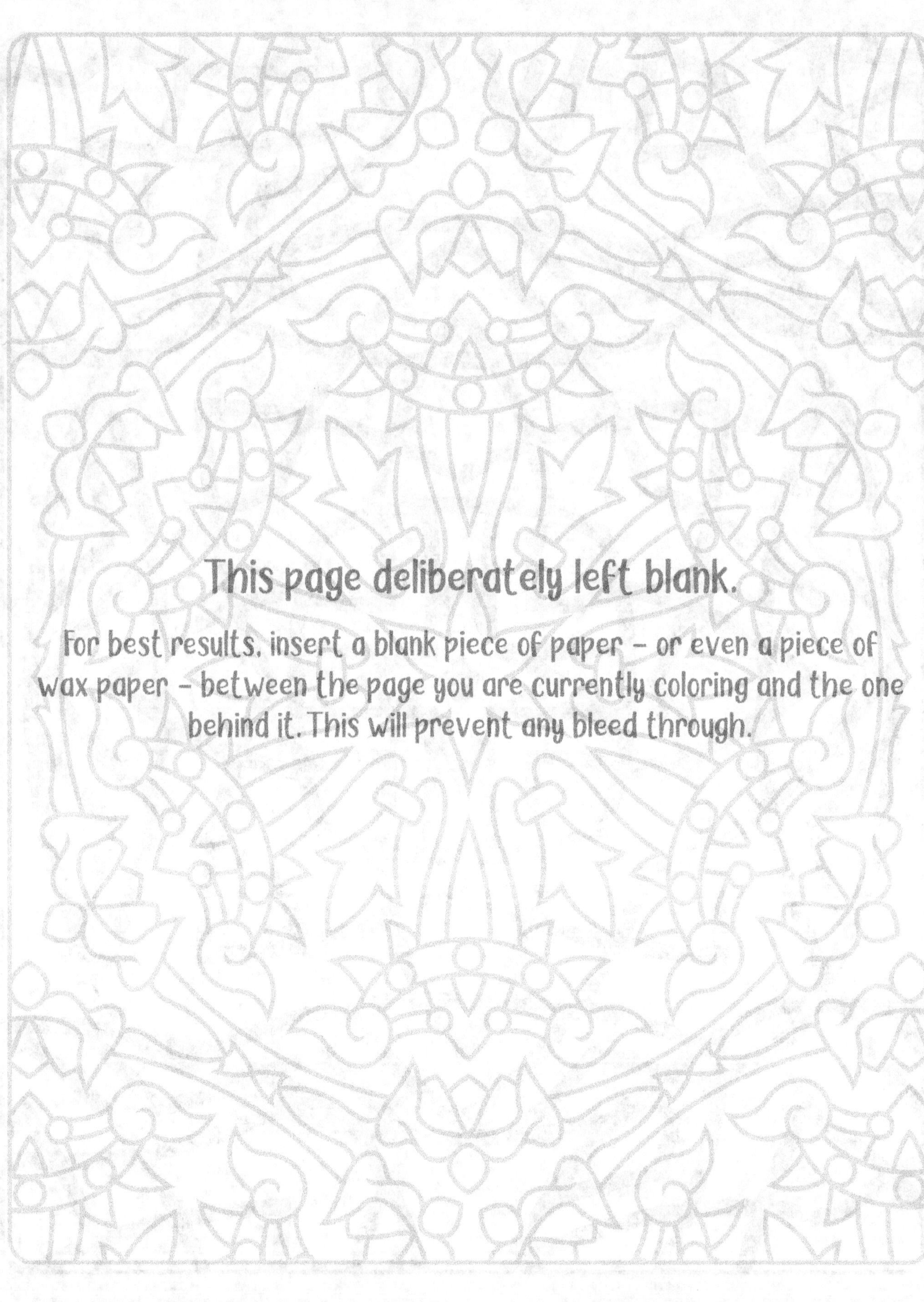

This page deliberately left blank.

For best results, insert a blank piece of paper – or even a piece of wax paper – between the page you are currently coloring and the one behind it. This will prevent any bleed through.

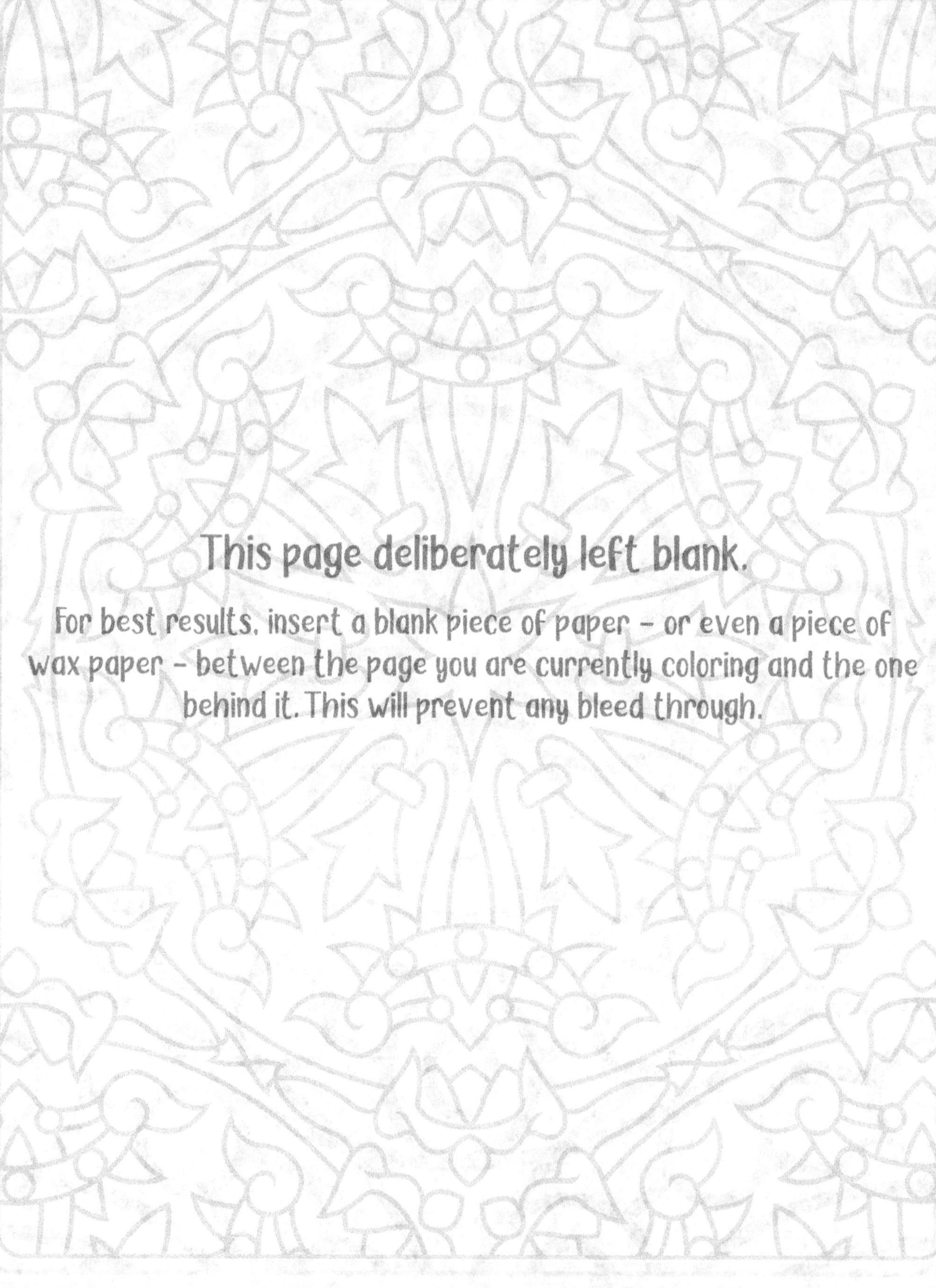

This page deliberately left blank.

For best results, insert a blank piece of paper – or even a piece of wax paper – between the page you are currently coloring and the one behind it. This will prevent any bleed through.

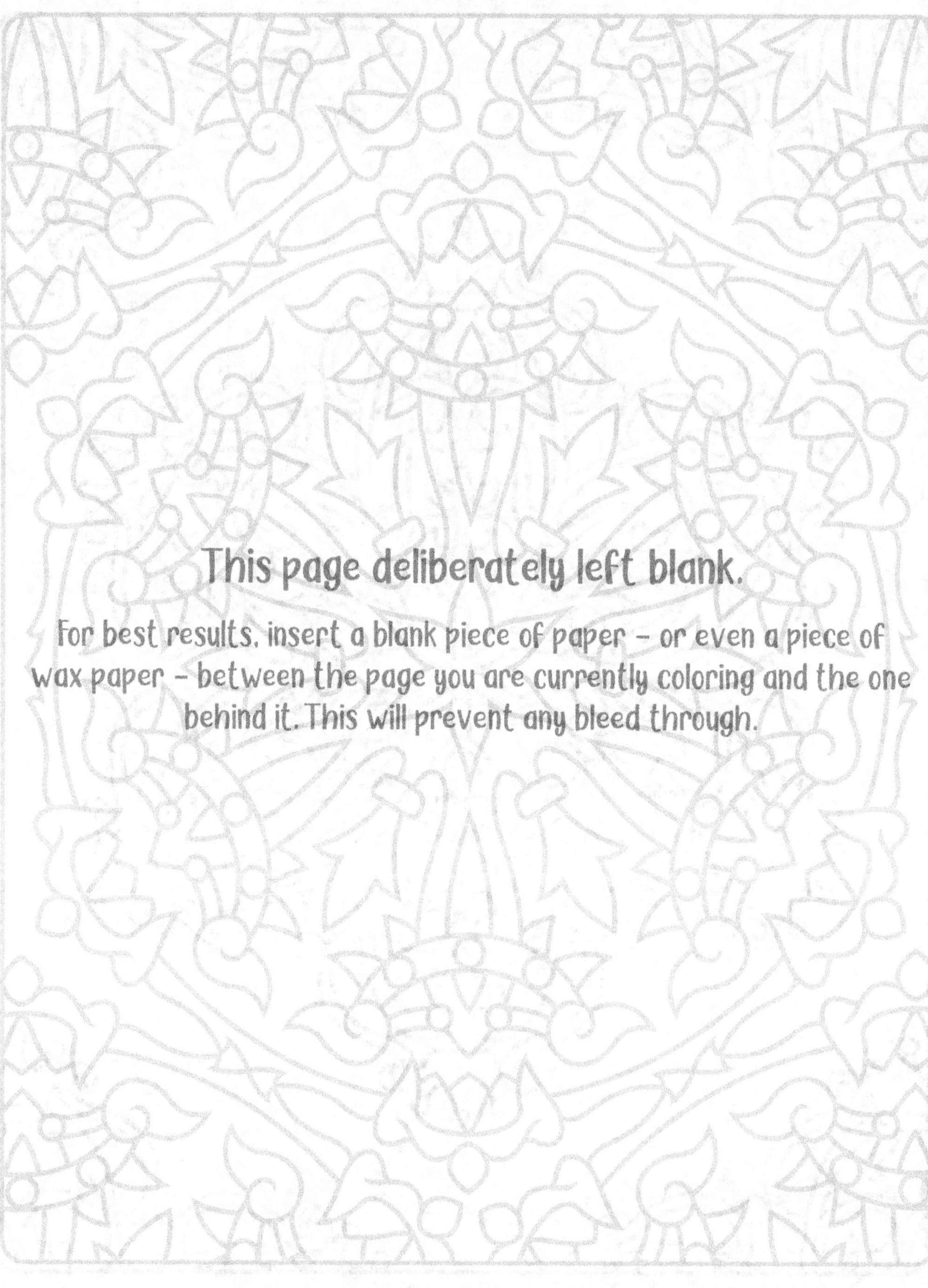

This page deliberately left blank.

For best results, insert a blank piece of paper – or even a piece of wax paper – between the page you are currently coloring and the one behind it. This will prevent any bleed through.

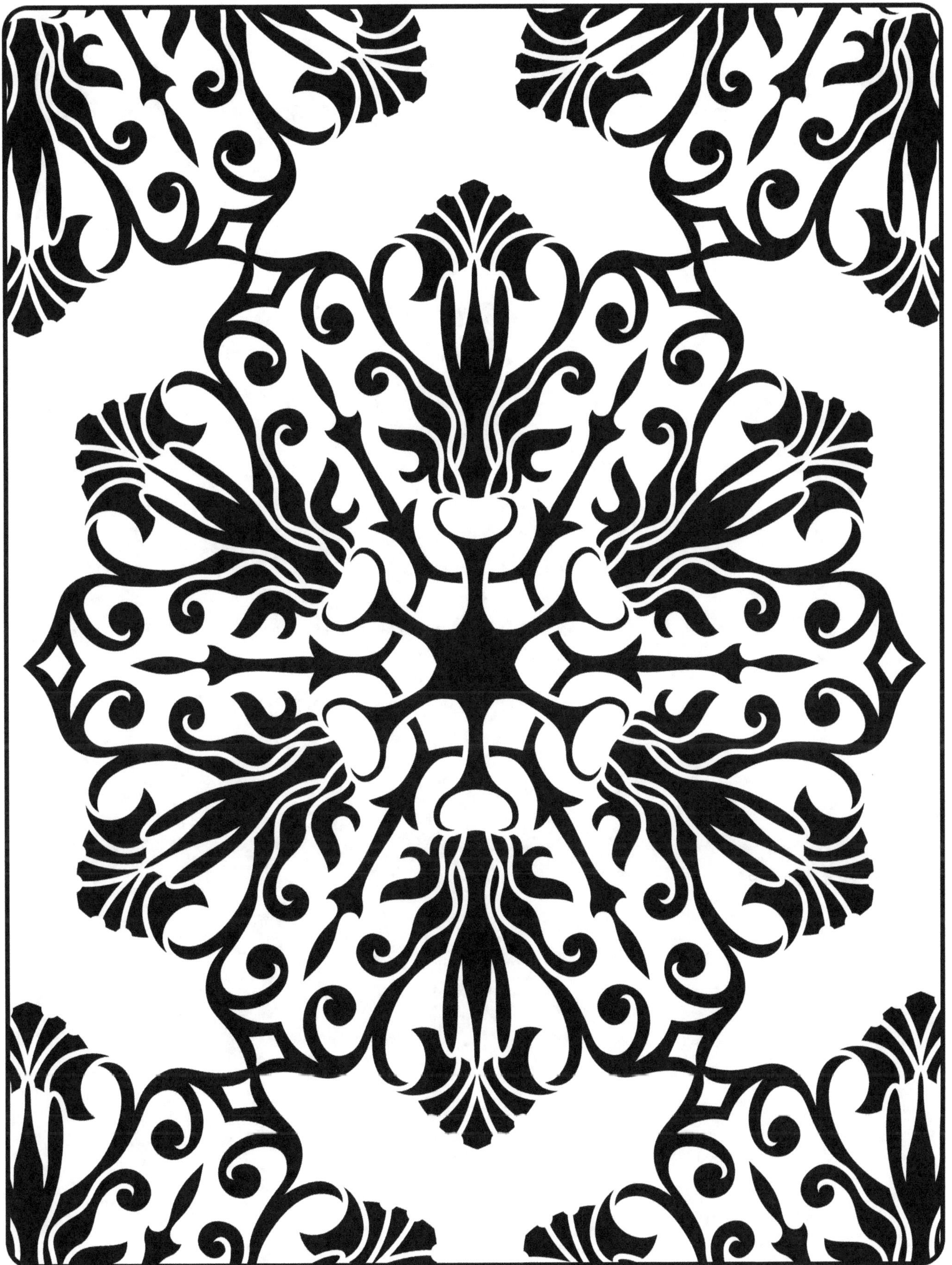

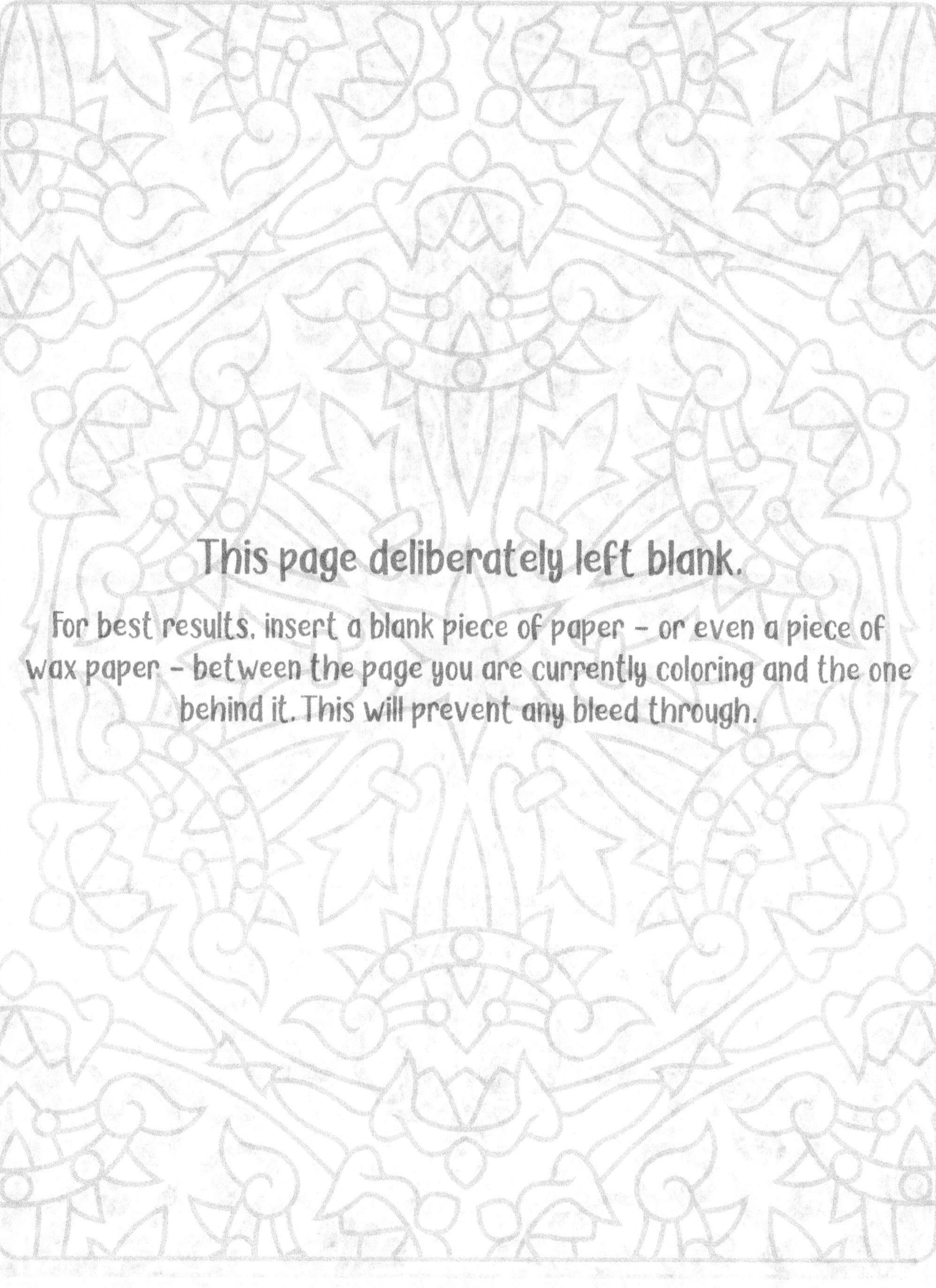

This page deliberately left blank.

For best results, insert a blank piece of paper - or even a piece of wax paper - between the page you are currently coloring and the one behind it. This will prevent any bleed through.

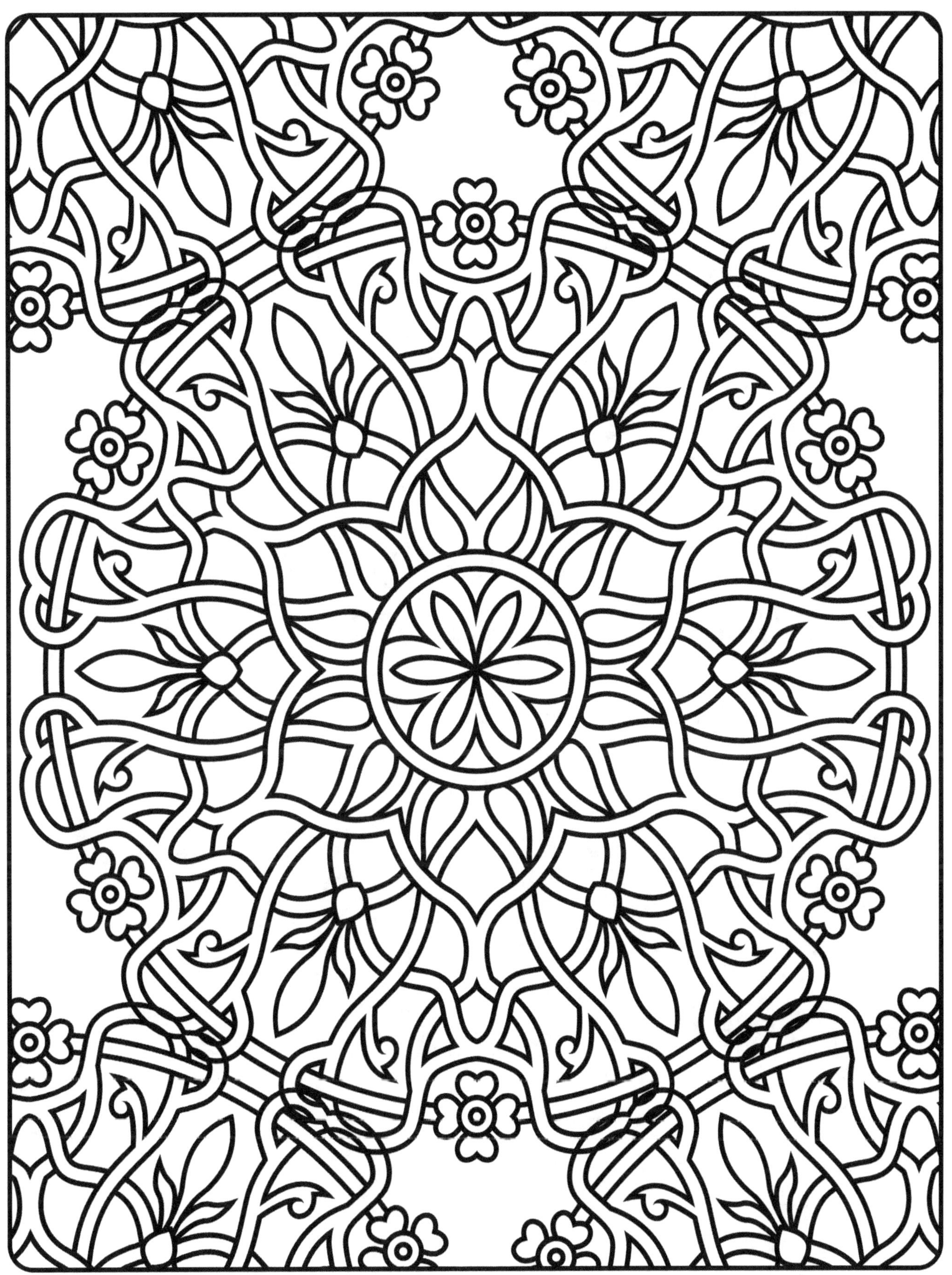

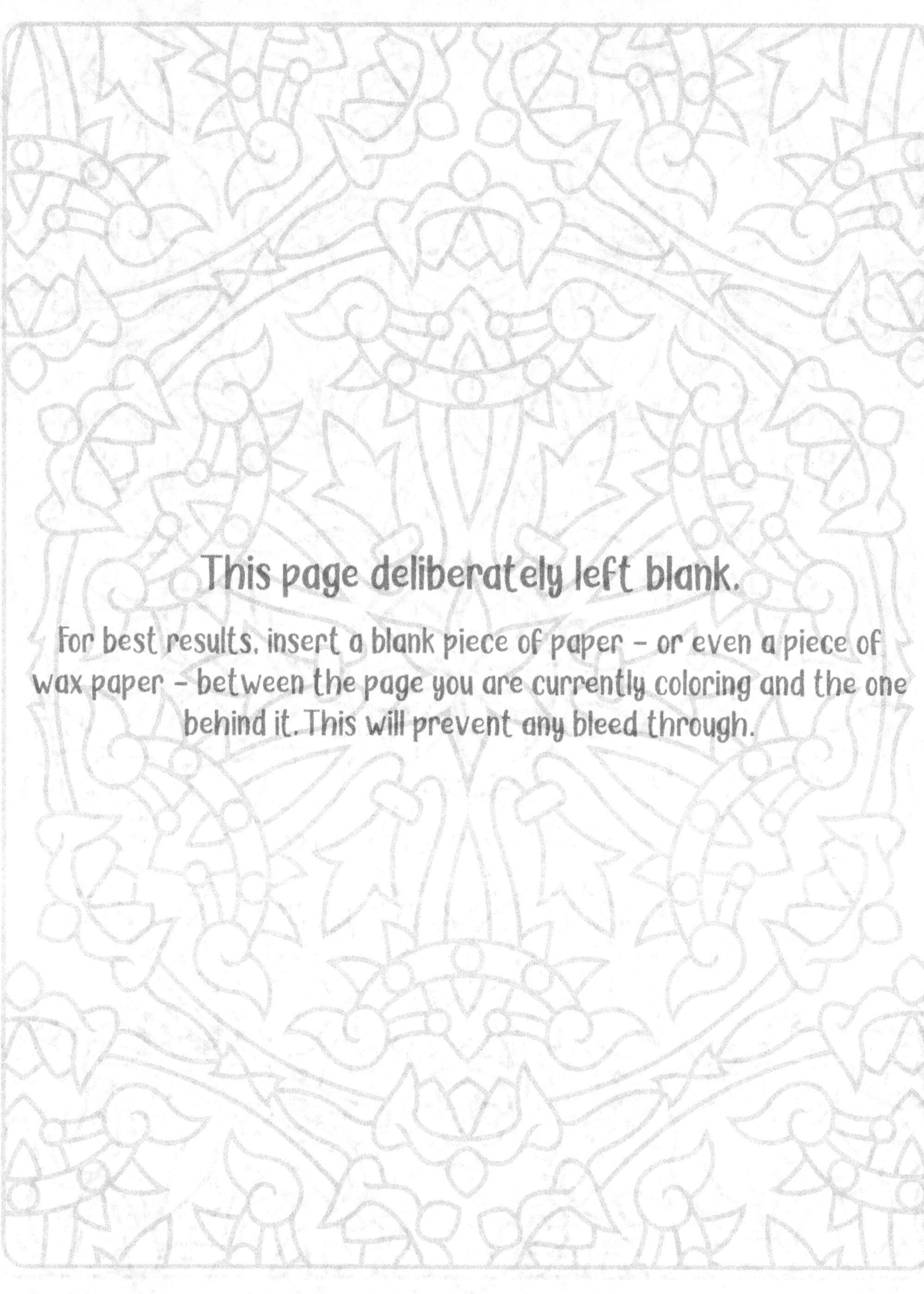

This page deliberately left blank.

For best results, insert a blank piece of paper – or even a piece of wax paper – between the page you are currently coloring and the one behind it. This will prevent any bleed through.

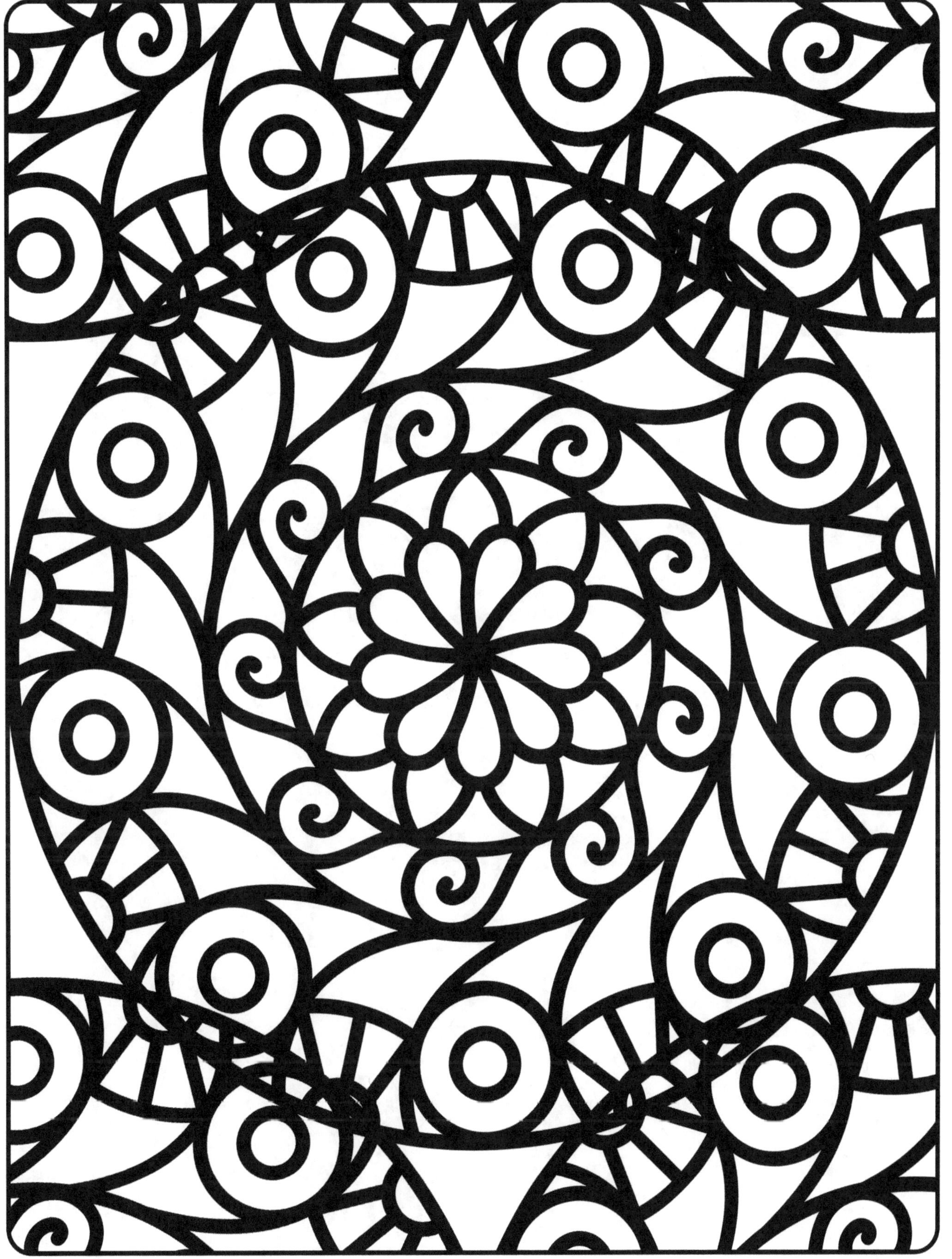

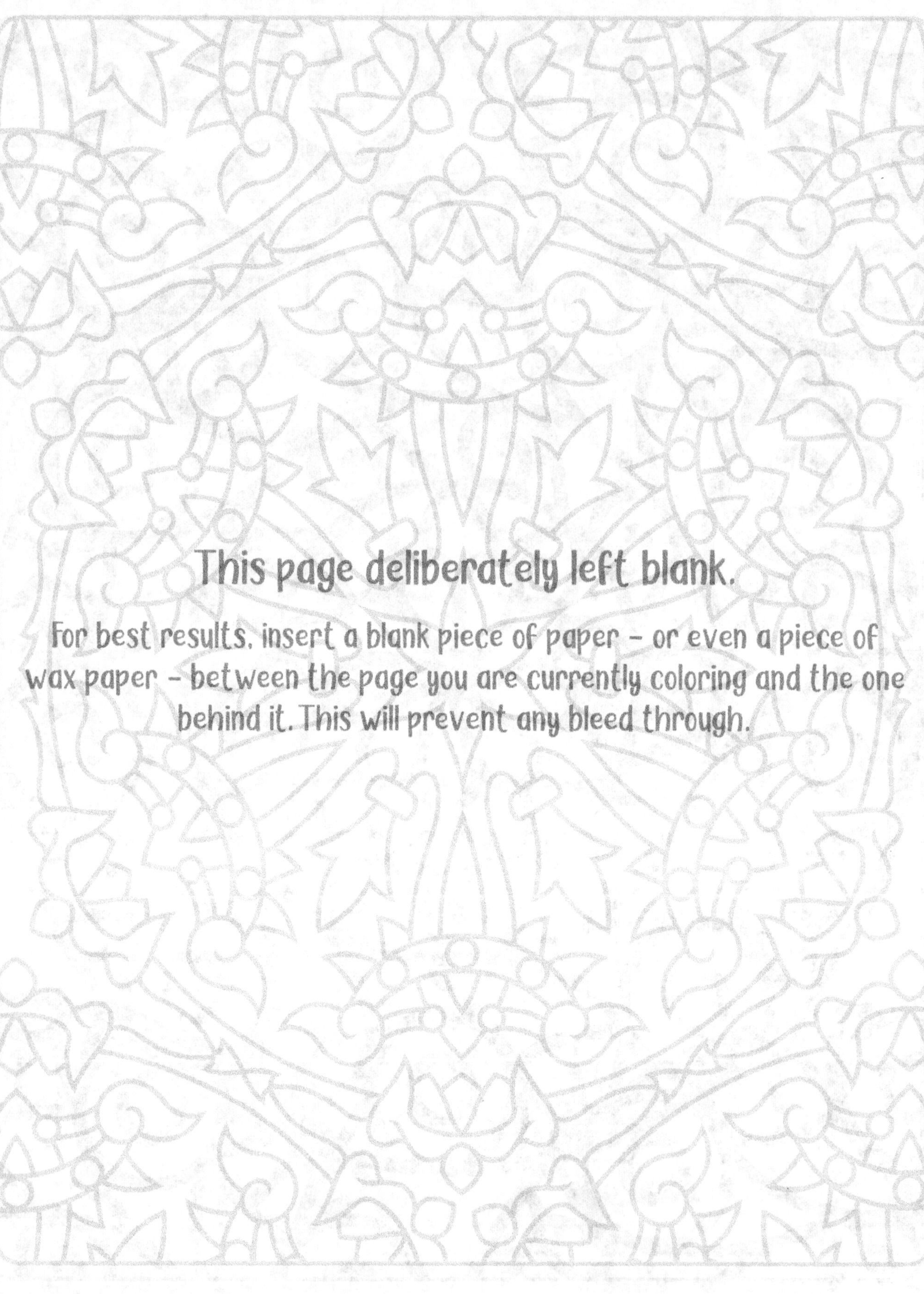

This page deliberately left blank.

For best results, insert a blank piece of paper – or even a piece of wax paper – between the page you are currently coloring and the one behind it. This will prevent any bleed through.

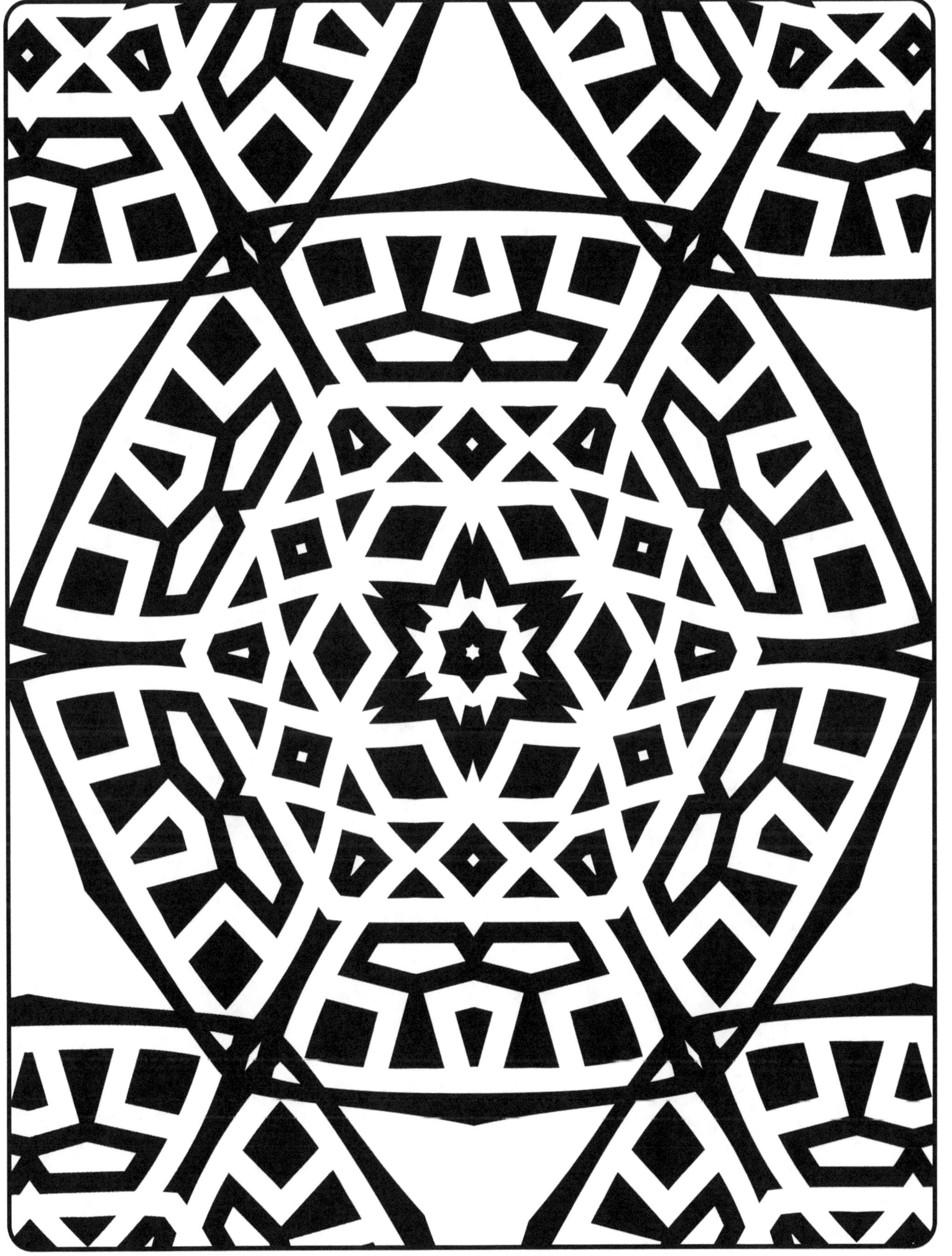

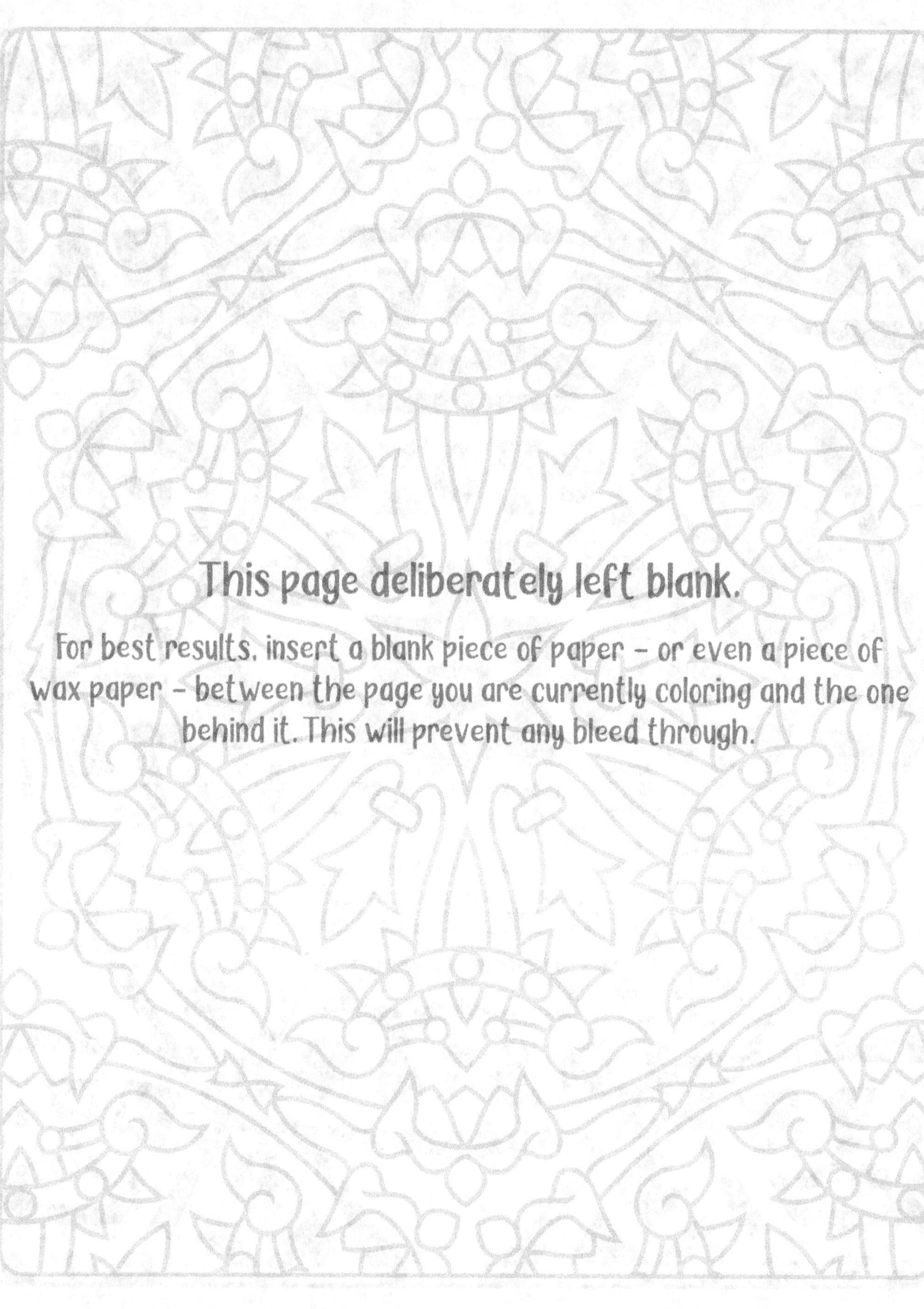

This page deliberately left blank.

For best results, insert a blank piece of paper – or even a piece of wax paper – between the page you are currently coloring and the one behind it. This will prevent any bleed through.

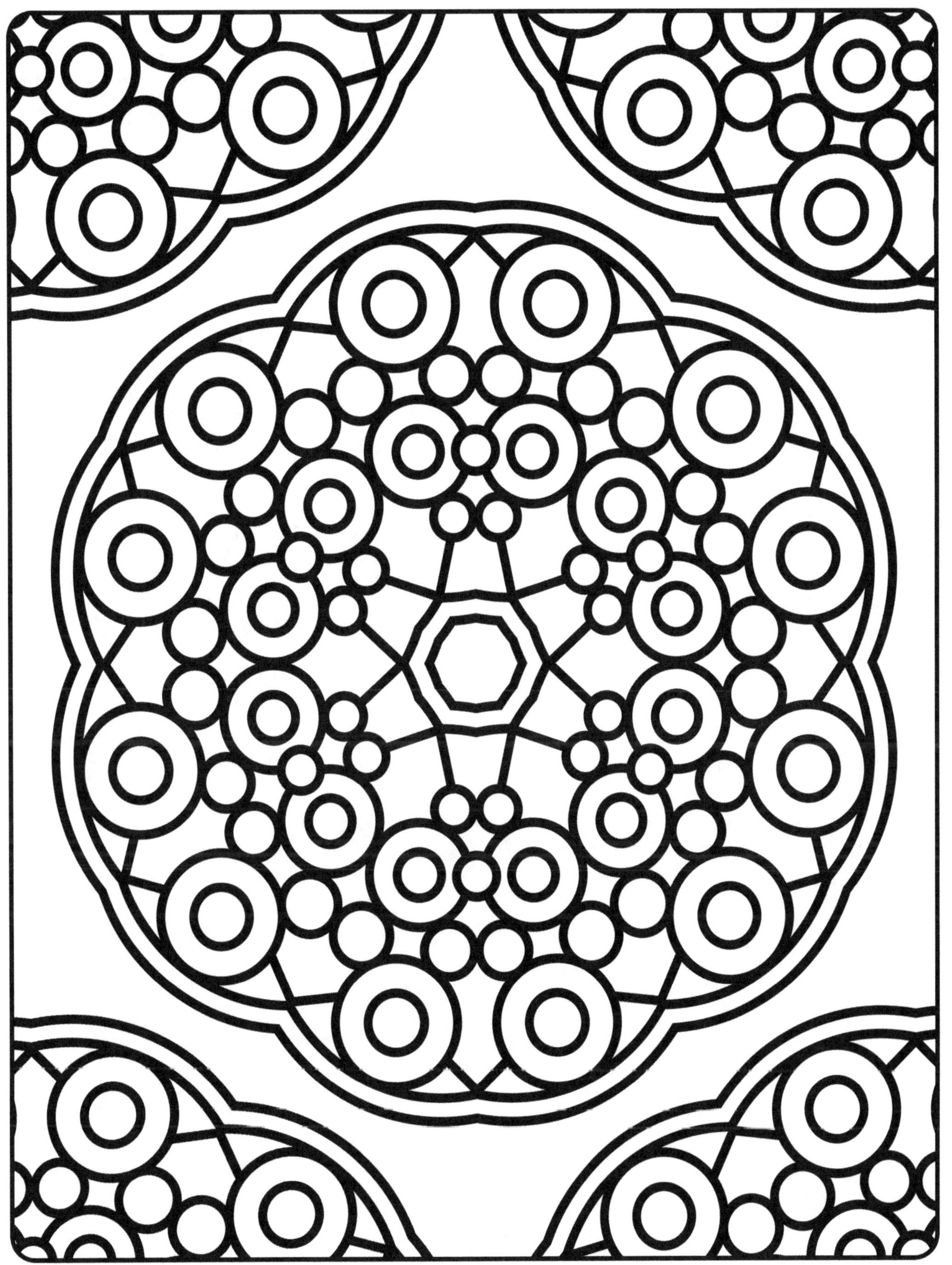

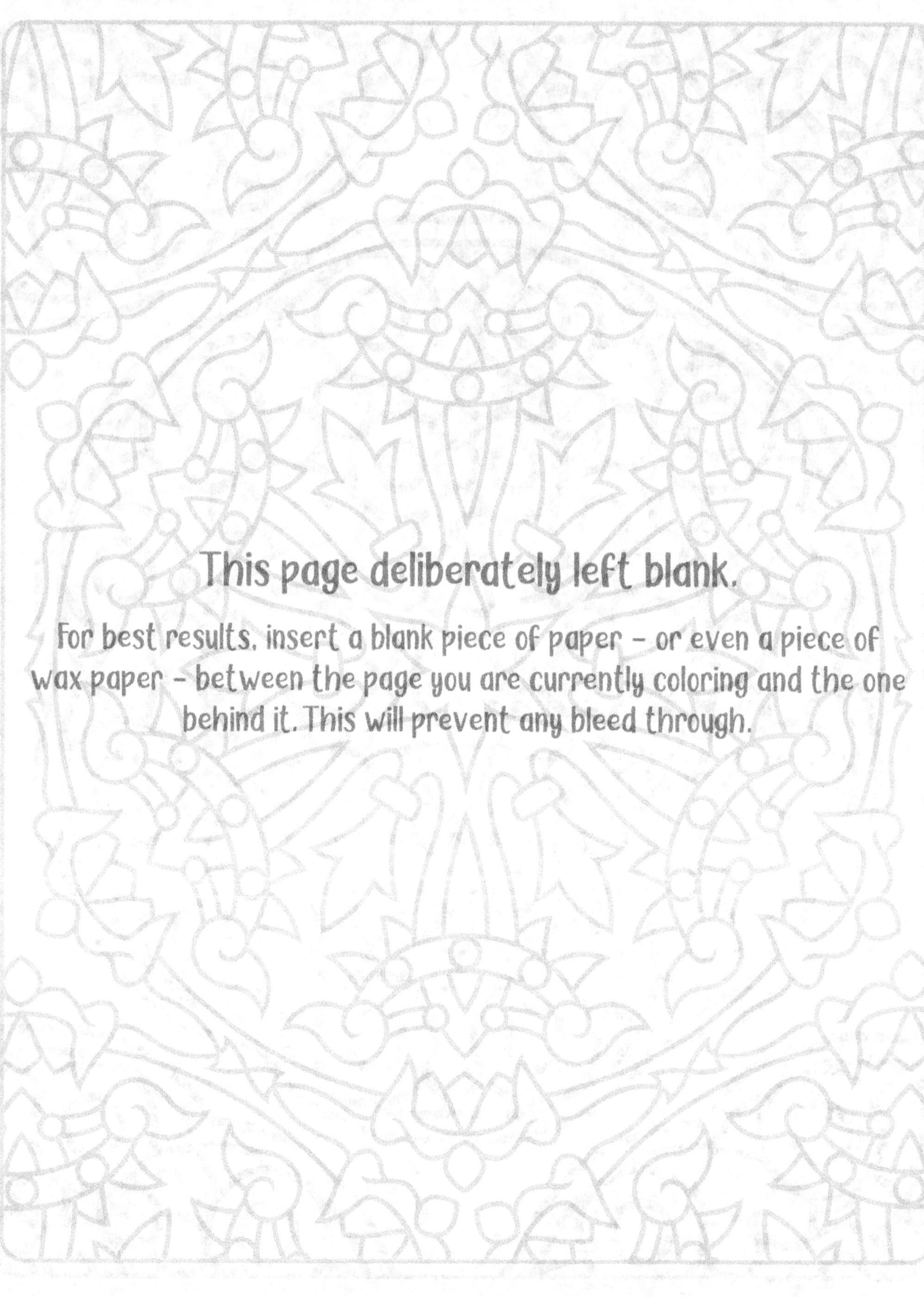

This page deliberately left blank.

For best results, insert a blank piece of paper – or even a piece of wax paper – between the page you are currently coloring and the one behind it. This will prevent any bleed through.

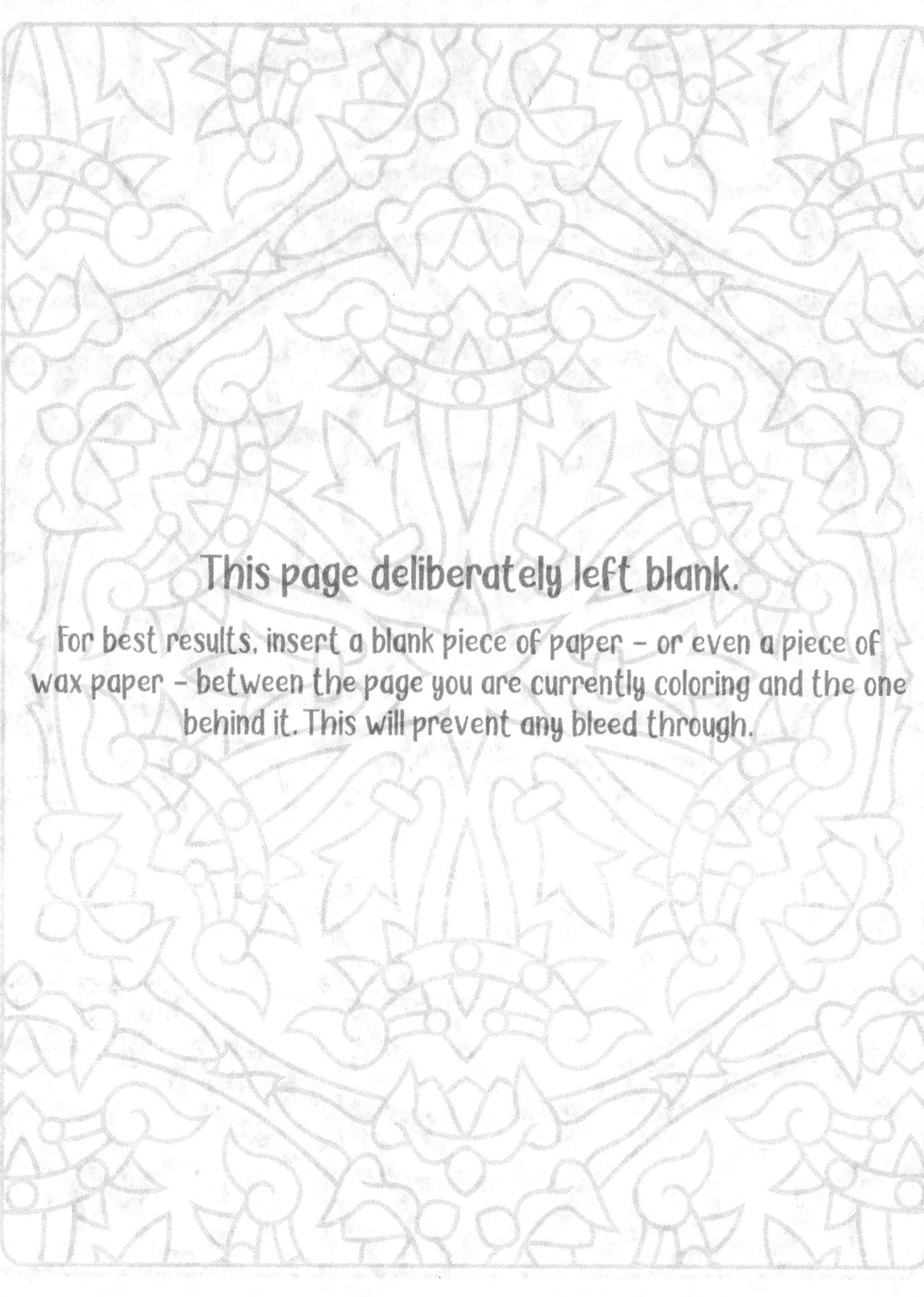

This page deliberately left blank.

For best results, insert a blank piece of paper – or even a piece of wax paper – between the page you are currently coloring and the one behind it. This will prevent any bleed through.

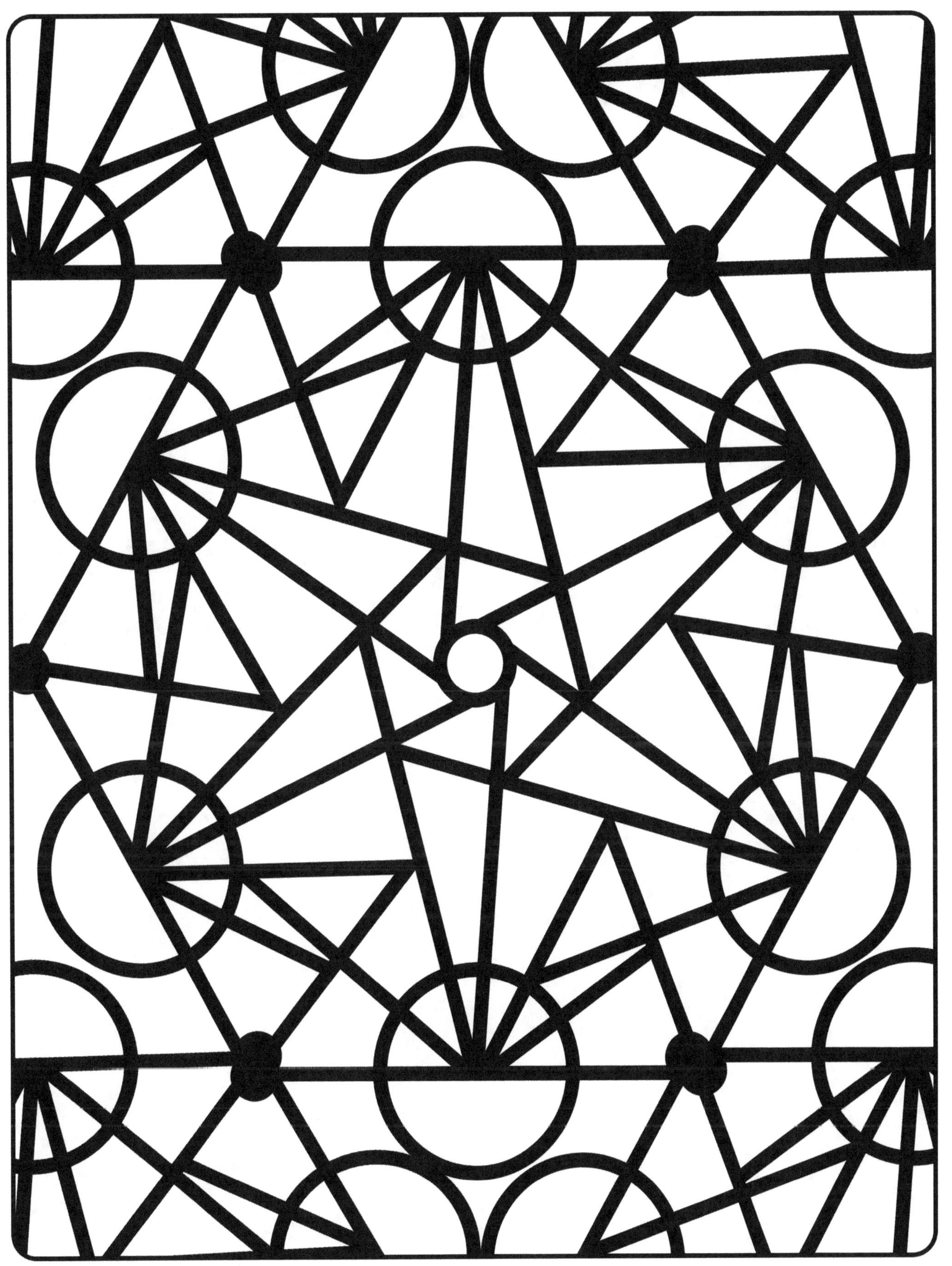

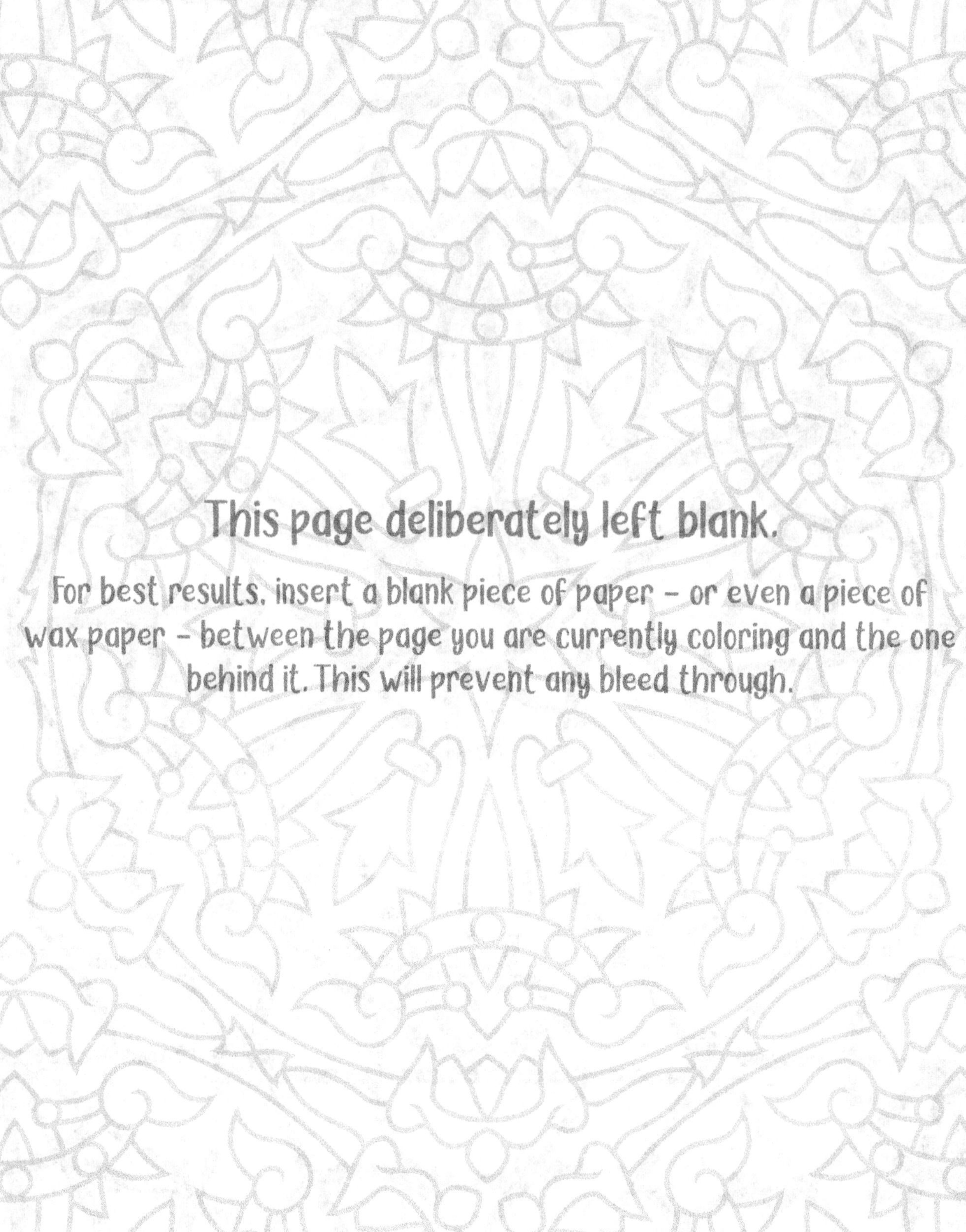

This page deliberately left blank.

For best results, insert a blank piece of paper – or even a piece of wax paper – between the page you are currently coloring and the one behind it. This will prevent any bleed through.

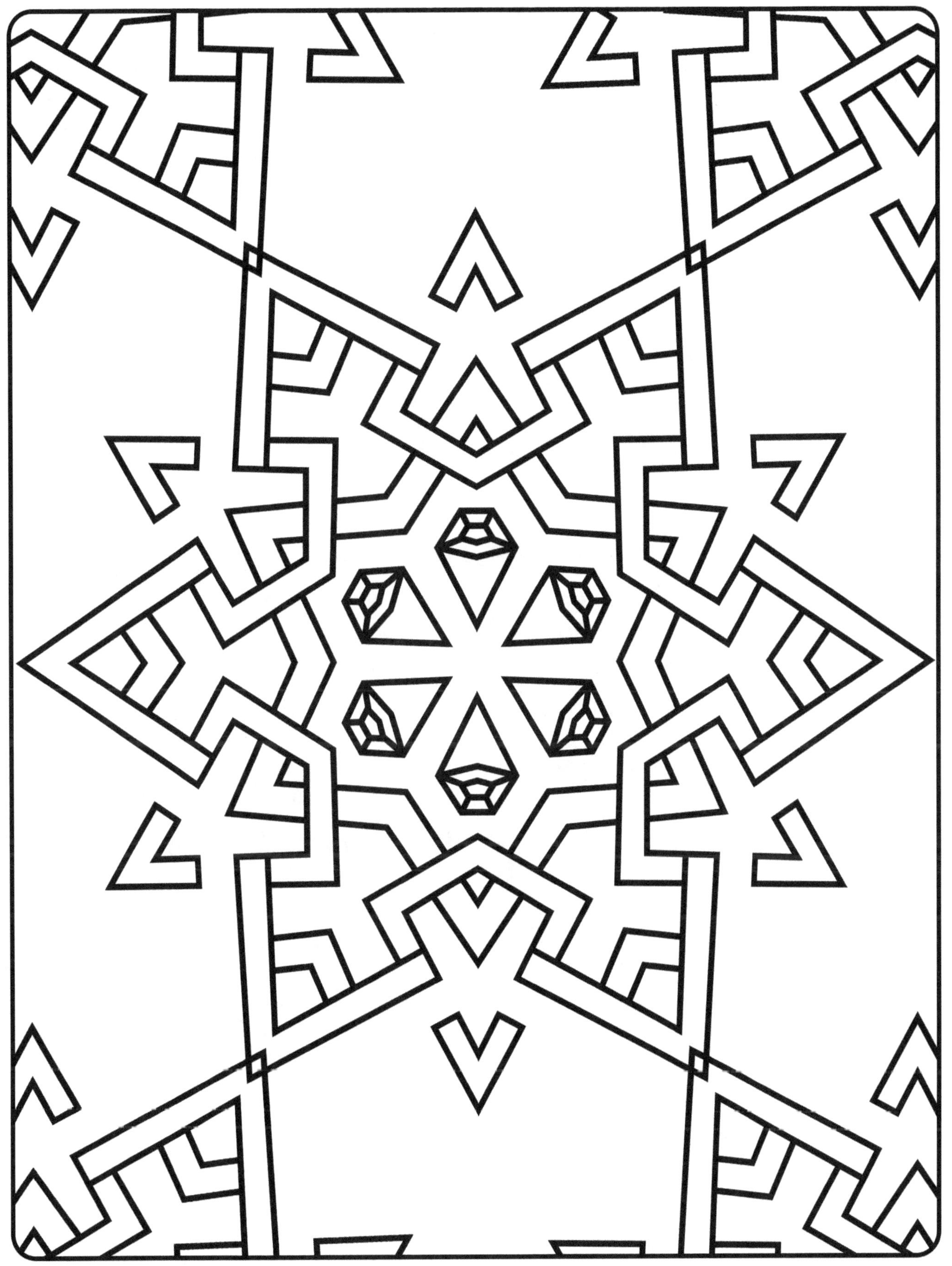

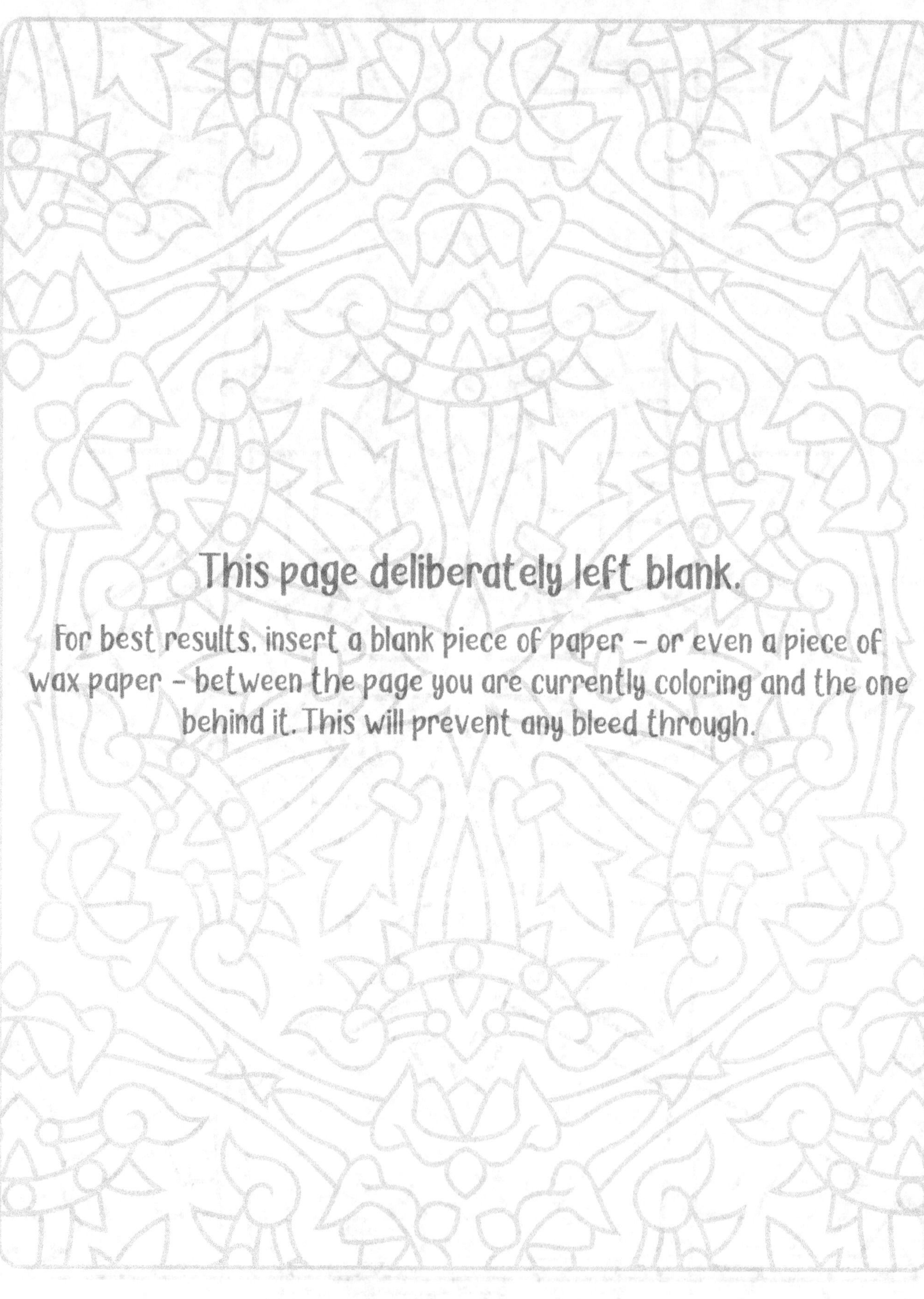

This page deliberately left blank.

For best results, insert a blank piece of paper – or even a piece of wax paper – between the page you are currently coloring and the one behind it. This will prevent any bleed through.

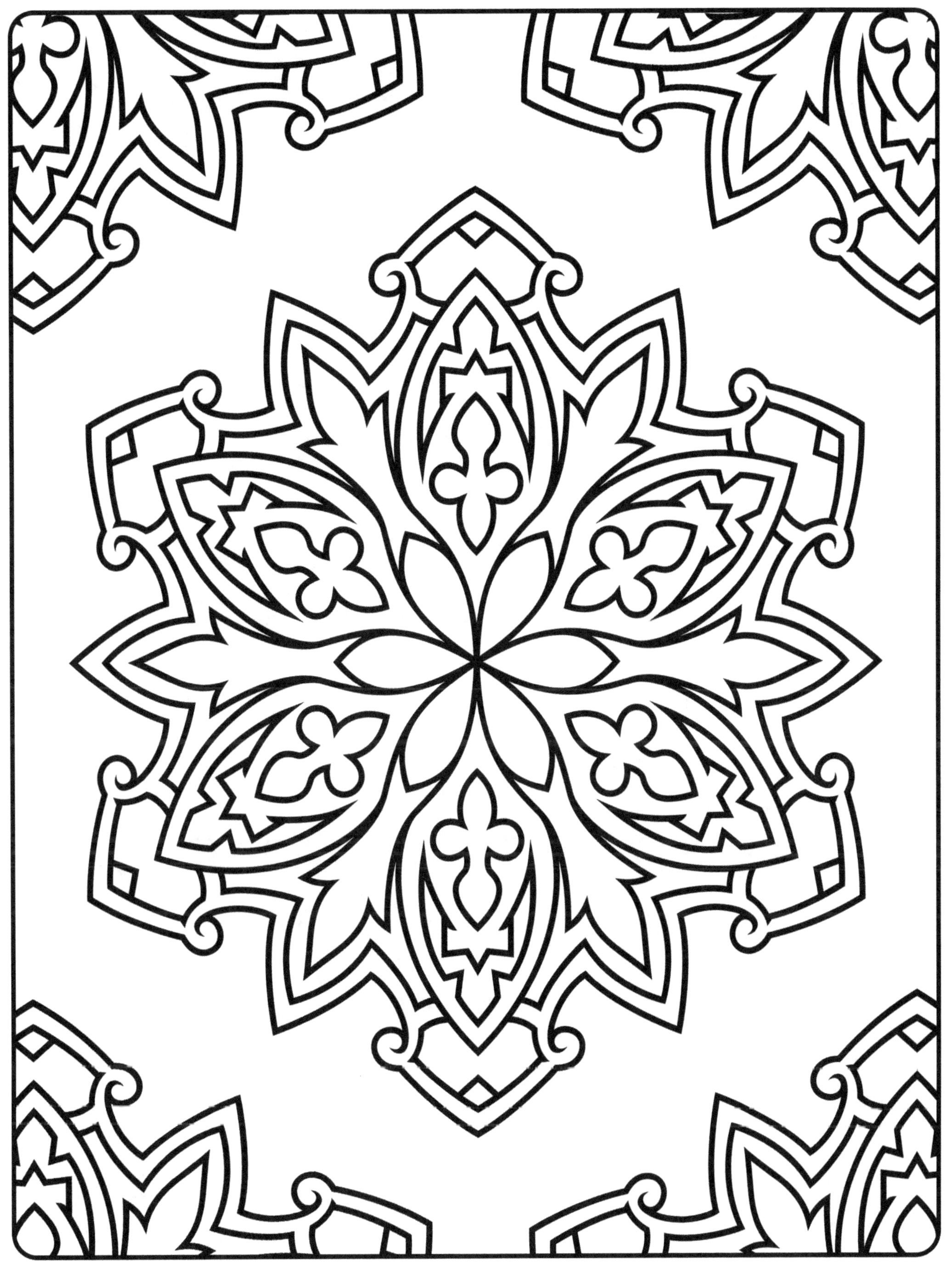

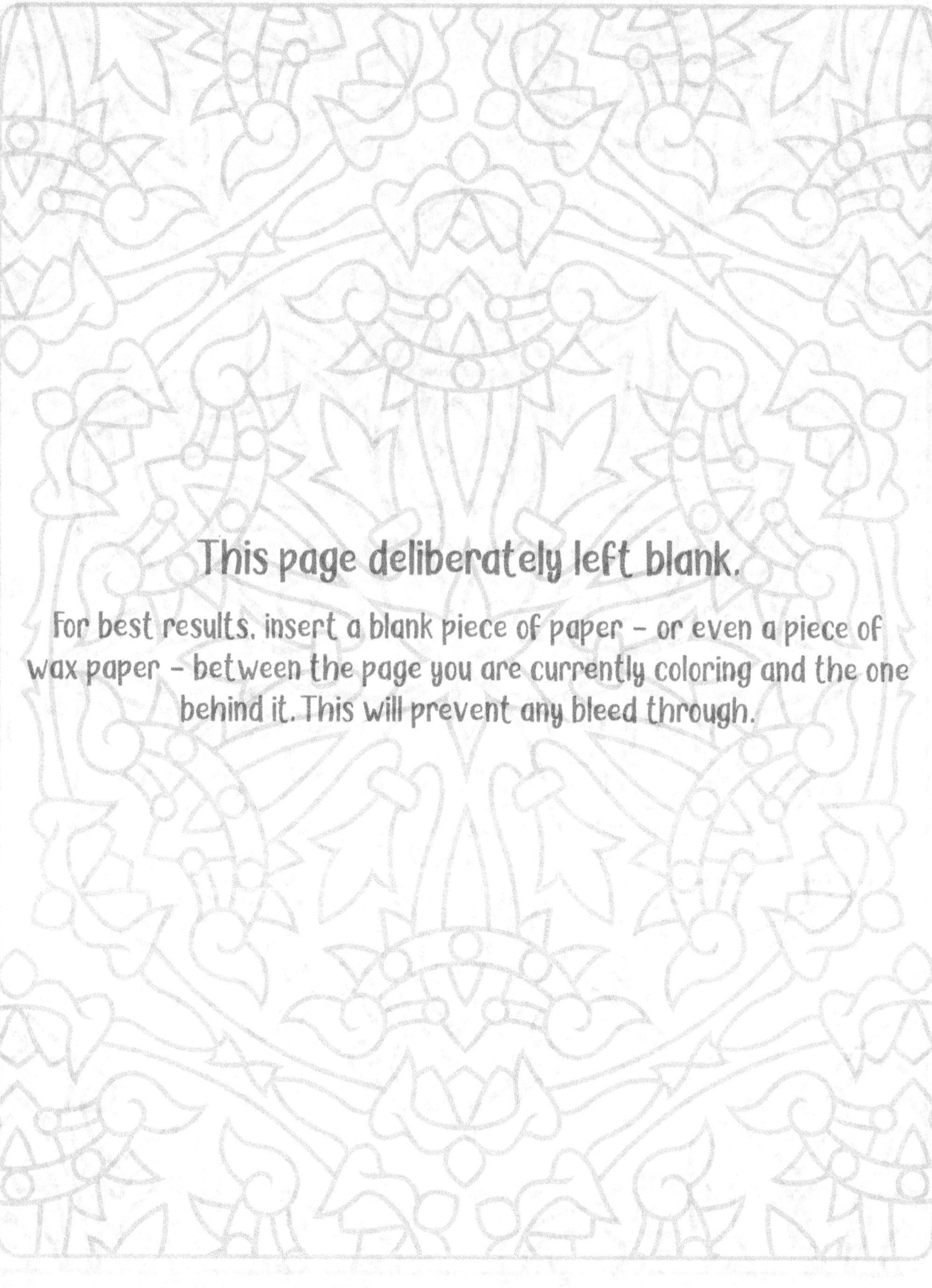

This page deliberately left blank.

For best results, insert a blank piece of paper – or even a piece of wax paper – between the page you are currently coloring and the one behind it. This will prevent any bleed through.

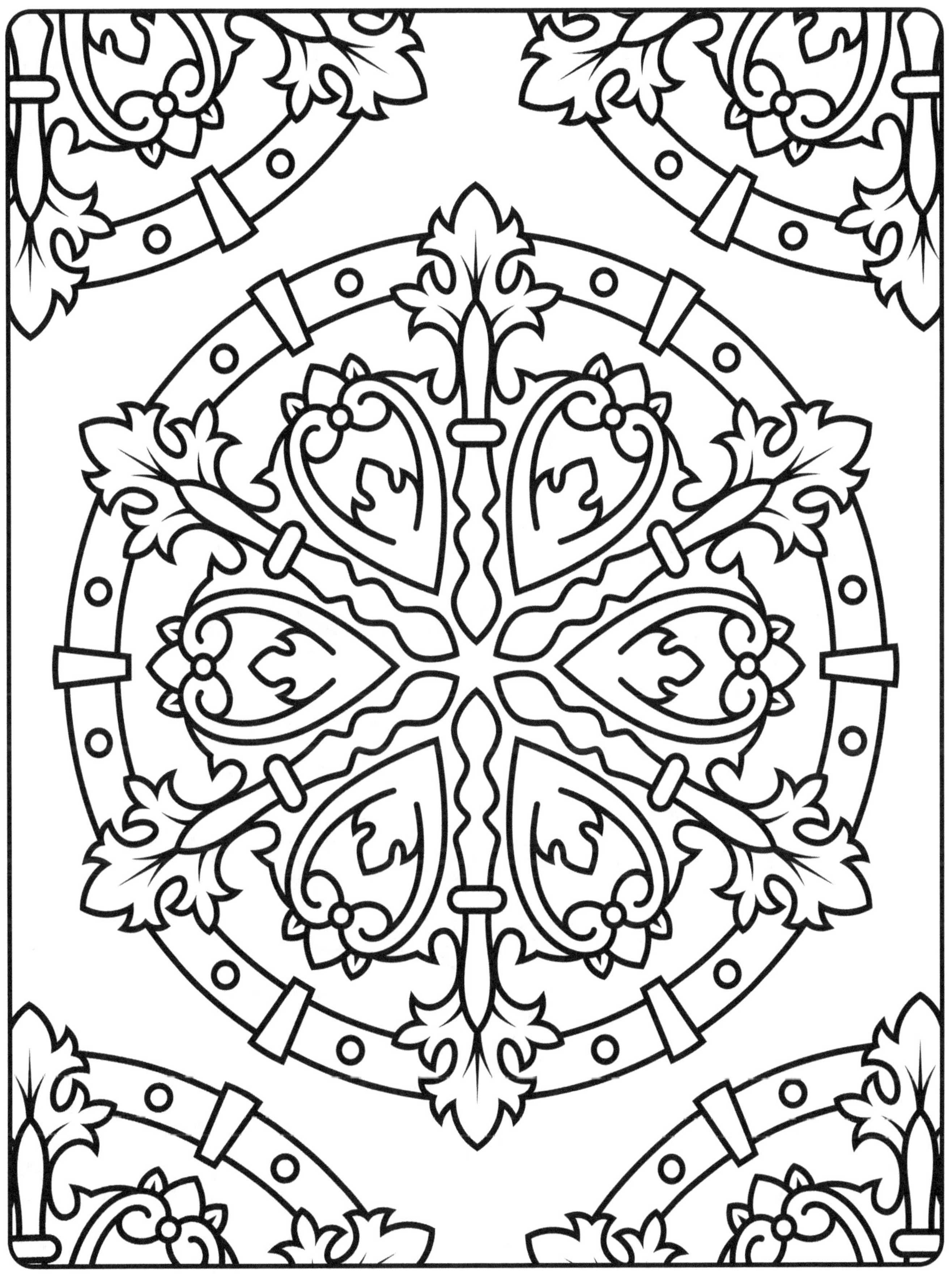

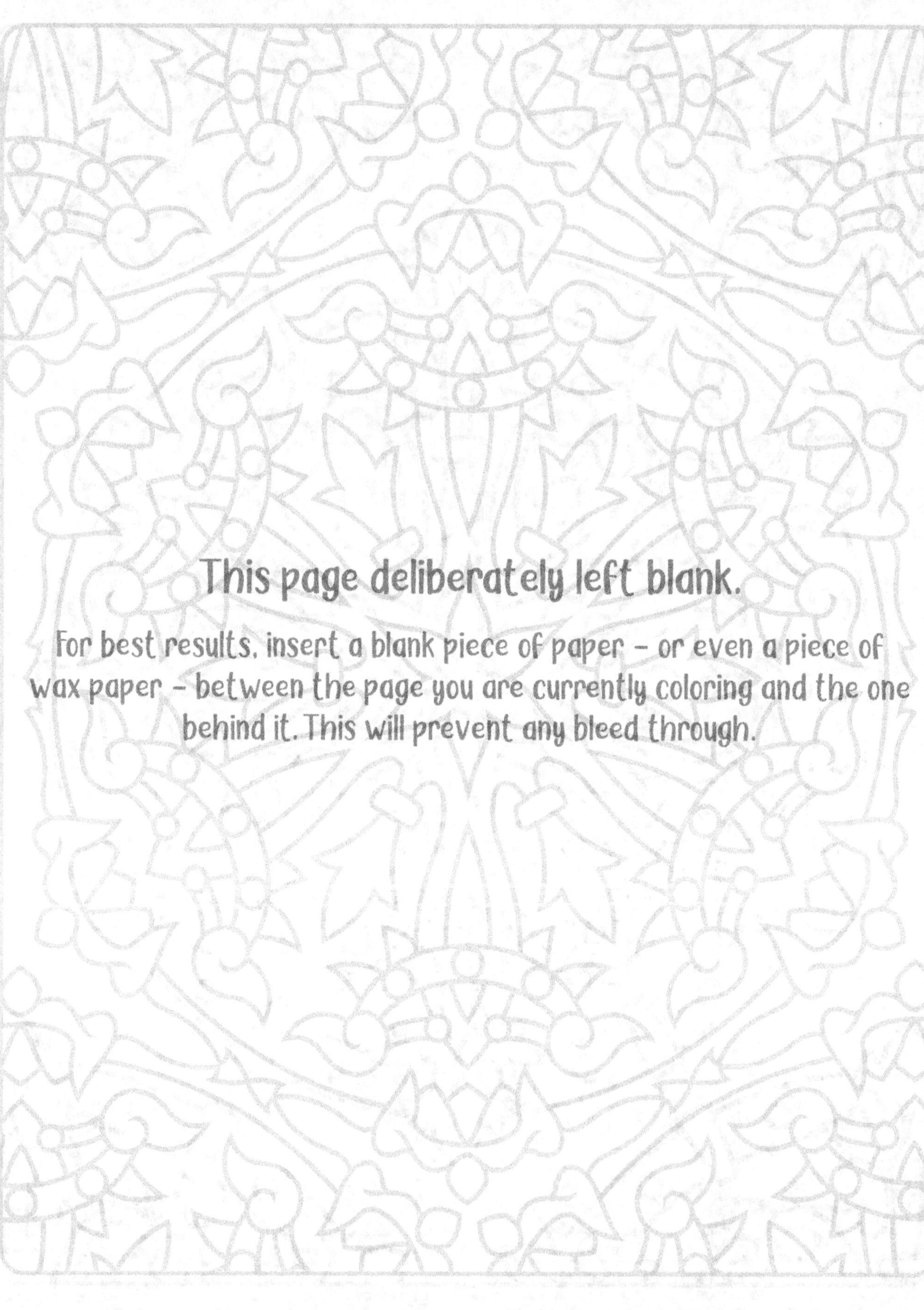

This page deliberately left blank.

For best results, insert a blank piece of paper – or even a piece of wax paper – between the page you are currently coloring and the one behind it. This will prevent any bleed through.

Also by Katherine Mariaca-Sullivan:

I Think of My Sister: A Keepsake Prompt Journal
She is Woman: A Quiet Little Diary for Women
Magnificent Mandalas Adult Coloring Book 1
Magnificent Mandalas Adult Coloring Book 2
Magnificent Mandalas Adult Coloring Book 3
Magnificent Mandalas Adult Coloring Book 4
Flower Mandala Adult Coloring Book – Black Background Edition
Flower Mandalas Adult Coloring Book
Zen & The Art of Coloring Yourself Calm: Winter Holiday Edition
Zen & The Art of Coloring Yourself Calm: Ocean Life Edition
Water from Stone – a Novel
The Stages of Grace – a Novel
When a Loved One Dies
The Complication of Sisters – Collected Stories & Drawings
If You Were a Critter
Is Ruby Jane REALLY a Pain? (with Heather Maurice-Stirnweis)

Visit KatMariacaStudio.com for greeting cards & gifts by the author

Follow Kat at:

@KatMariacaStudio
facebook.com/KatMariacaStudio

Looking for More Great Coloring Books for Adults?

I've got you covered. Simply copy and paste the ID number of my coloring books into Amazon's search bar and take off on your next great Zen adventure. Follow my Amazon page to keep up-to-date on my newest coloring book releases - and to learn about my novels, journals and other exciting books.
Happy coloring!

- Kat
Katherine Mariaca-Sullivan
Amazon Author Page ID: B005A43C1K

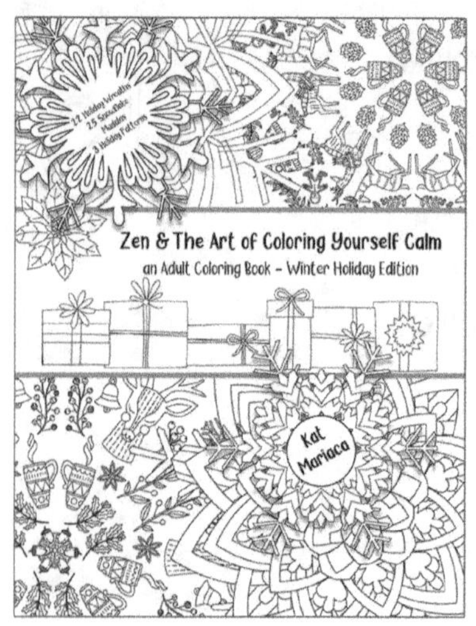

1940892074

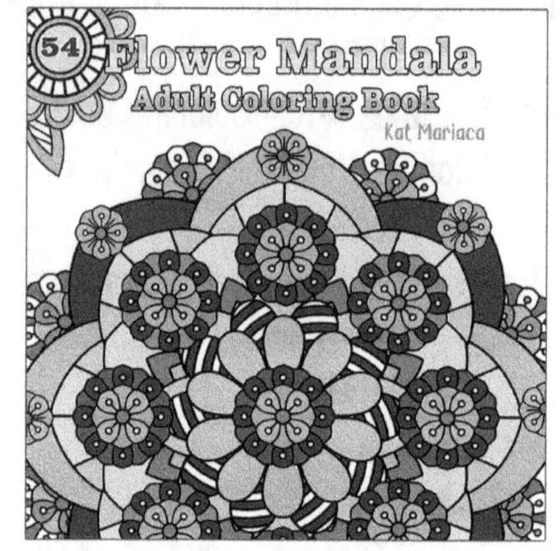

1940892155

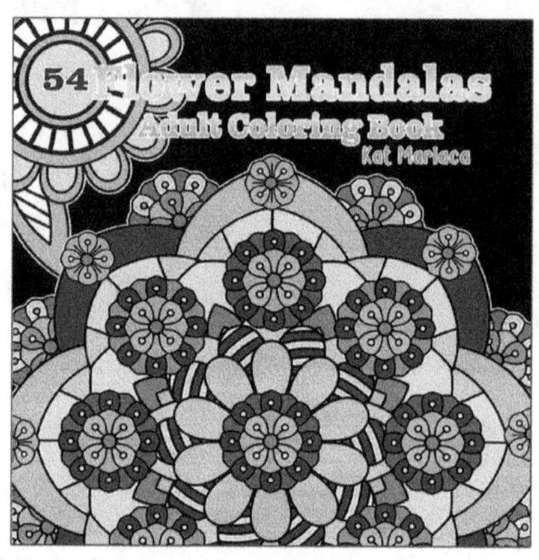

4294351780

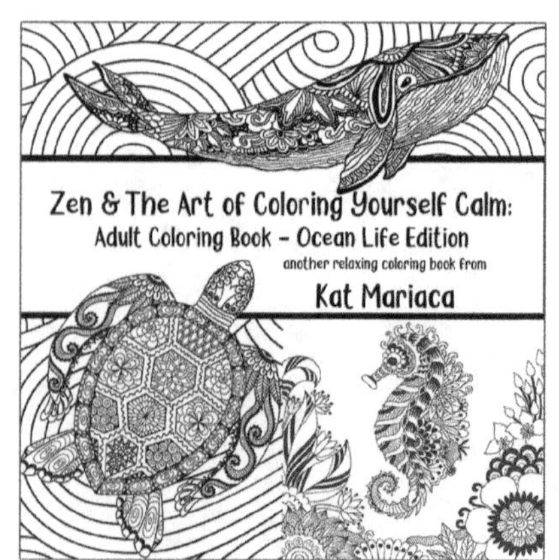

1940892147

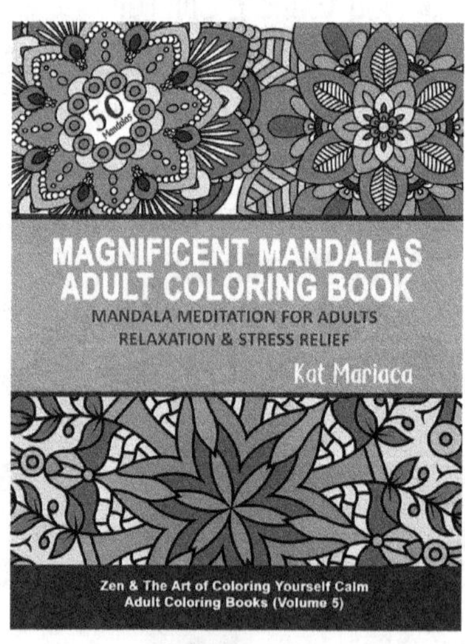

1940892198

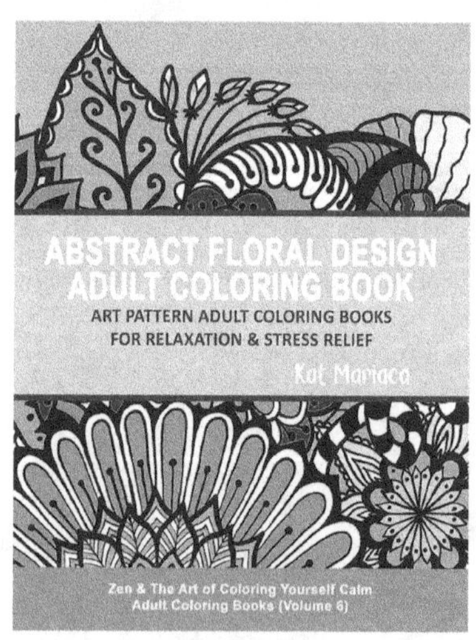

1940892236

www.ingramcontent.com/pod-product-compliance
Lightning Source LLC
LaVergne TN
LVHW080312110826

845155LV00023B/119
* 9 7 8 1 9 4 0 8 9 2 2 5 2 *